THE FINANCE CRISIS AND RESCUE:
What Went Wrong? Why? What Lessons Can Be Learned?

The 2008 global financial crisis affects everyone, but its root causes and potential cures are confusing to many. This compilation of expert views from the University of Toronto's Rotman School of Management explores what went wrong and why, and considers the lessons that these events can teach businesspeople, policy makers, and the general public alike.

The Finance Crisis and Rescue features essays from ten leading Rotman professors and renowned journalist Michael Hlinka, and includes a foreword by Rotman Dean Roger Martin. These intellectual leaders from the front lines of business thinking tackle the subject from a number of angles, analysing the crisis from the perspective of their diverse backgrounds in fields such as structured finance, behavioural finance, value investing, pension management, risk management, corporate governance, public policy, and leadership.

A timely and considered response to current events, *The Finance Crisis and Rescue* will be of interest to anyone concerned with recent global financial developments.

THE

FINANCE
CRISIS
AND **RESCUE**

what went wrong? why?
what lessons can be learned?

UNIVERSITY OF TORONTO PRESS
Toronto Buffalo London

www.utppublishing.com
Printed in Canada

ISBN 978-1-4426-4012-2 (cloth)
ISBN 978-1-4426-0987-7 (paper)

Printed on acid-free paper

Publication cataloguing information is available from Library and
Archives Canada.

University of Toronto Press acknowledges the financial assistance to its
publishing program of the Canada Council for the Arts and the Ontario
Arts Council.

University of Toronto Press acknowledges the financial support for its
publishing activities of the Government of Canada through the Book
Publishing Industry Development Program (BPIDP).

Contents

Foreword   vii
Roger Martin

1 LEADERSHIP

**Rescuing the Global Financial System: The Failure of
American Leadership**   3
Jim Fisher

2 DERIVATIVES AND RISK MANAGEMENT

**The Financial Crisis of 2007: Another Case of Irrational
Exuberance**   17
John Hull

3 STRUCTURED FINANCE

**Subprime, Market Meltdown, and Learning from the
Past**   17
Laurence Booth

4 VALUE INVESTING

Value Investing in the Crisis: How Margins of Safety Melted Away   53

Eric Kirzner

5 FINANCIAL ANALYSIS

Integrative Thinking (or Lack of) and the Current Crisis   69

Ramy Elitzur

6 BUSINESS ECONOMICS

The Financial Crisis of 2008 and the 'Real' Economy: Damage but Not Disaster   81

Peter Dungan

7 INTERNATIONAL BUSINESS

Global Lessons from the 2008 Financial Crisis   95

Wendy Dobson

8 CORPORATE GOVERNANCE

Where Were the Directors?   107

David Beatty

9 BEHAVIOURAL FINANCE

The Influence of Investor Behaviour   123

Lisa Kramer

10 PENSION MANAGEMENT

**Looking across the Abyss: Pension Design and Management
in the Twenty-First Century** 137
Keith Ambachtsheer

11 PUBLIC POLICY

**Carts and Horses and Horses and Carts: How Public Policy
Led to the Subprime Disaster** 149
Michael Hlinka

Contributors 163

Foreword

If someone had told you five years ago that some bad mortgages in the suburbs of Florida could lead to the bankruptcy of a country like Iceland, you wouldn't be the only one not to have believed it. Fast forward to today, and there are few doubters left as to how incredibly interconnected – and perversely incentive-driven – our global economy has become.

I am far from the only one who has warned of the negative effects of financial incentives. As I wrote in *Rotman Magazine* in the fall of 2004, just as animal trainers can use the right set of incentives to get lions to jump through flaming hoops or elephants to walk on their hind legs, monetary incentives can get people to engage in 'unnatural' behaviour of all sorts. As we have seen of late, even the smartest and most experienced among them can turn a blind eye when the short-term incentive is right.

Clearly, central aspects of the finance industry are badly broken. The system must be redesigned so that it brings out something closer to the best in human behaviour rather than what appears to have been the worst. On the pages that follow, the finance crisis and rescue are viewed through a wide-angle lens by eleven thought leaders from the front lines of business thinking. Covering everything from credit risk to value investing to leadership, our experts tackle the broken model and proposed rescue and provide insight for moving ahead.

In the end, the treatment required to cure this unhealthy system may be deceptively simple: to produce more beneficial results for stakeholders and for society at large, firms must lower their expectations of monetary incentives and be more cognizant about setting them within a context that reduces the tendency for extremes of behaviour.

At the Rotman School of Management, we place great value on the ability to constructively face the tensions of opposing models. Instead of choosing one model at the expense of the other, we are teaching leaders how to generate creative resolutions with new-to-the-world models. We hope that, by learning more about where the current model failed and why, we can all take away important lessons that will allow us to shape our world for the better.

As a wise person once said, those who fail to learn from the mistakes of their predecessors are destined to repeat them.

Let the learning – and the healing – begin.

Roger Martin
Dean, Rotman School of Management
University of Toronto
November 2008

THE FINANCE CRISIS AND RESCUE

1

LEADERSHIP

Rescuing the Global Financial System:
The Failure of American Leadership

Jim Fisher

On 11 September 2001, two commercial airliners full of passengers were hijacked in the air and flown into the two buildings of the World Trade Center. A third was flown into the Pentagon and a fourth crashed into a field in Pennsylvania. I have a tape of CBC Radio's news coverage from that day. While reporters filed stories – disjointed bits and pieces on what seemed to be happening – anchors struggled to put the pieces together, to summarize what was known and to distinguish the known from the rumoured, to try to explain it, to put it in a context. There was confusion. But, wherever we were that day, whatever our personal connection to New York or Washington or to the people on the planes, we were transfixed. It would be fair to say that a good part of the world stopped and watched and listened in shock. And the media did what it does so well when we really need it. It made us all part of the community of the truly affected.

Listening to that tape later, I was struck by how often the producers turned to the elected leaders – the ones whom we have chosen – for comments on the events of the day. The prime minister, the leader of the Official Opposition, provincial premiers and mayors, all made public statements. Even reports that a public figure might make a statement became news. None of those people had any particular inside information to share, insight to provide, prospect to share. They were as much in the dark as the rest of us. Nonetheless, they were our leaders. Whether we voted for them or not, whether we even voted at all, at a time of crisis, our eyes turned to those who held leadership positions. Instinctively we had to hear from our leaders that day and in the days that followed.

In New York City, Rudolph Giuliani, a weary politician, waiting out the days until the end of his term, wounded by allegations of scandal in his administration, became a folk hero by his visibility in the smoke and fog. He gave New Yorkers, and the world, a sense that whatever happened and whatever else might happen, New York would get through it if they stayed together. He asked people to help their neighbours, to help and thank the police and fire departments. It was a simple message at a complex time. He was present. He was visible. He communicated and communicated and communicated.

There is extensive literature today on the intertwining of crisis and leadership. Crises are emotionally charged events and it seems to be a natural inclination of humans to look to our leaders at such times. But what do we look for? What do we expect? And what happens if our leaders go absent? Throughout the unfolding financial crisis we are living through now, we have seen a lack of basic crisis leadership and have experienced that failure in the continuing pessimism of global stock markets as one initiative after another comes forth, with seemingly little effect.

I will leave to others the question of whether the various actions taken by authorities around the world are appropriate or sufficient to end this crisis and begin the healing necessary to enable the global economy to function again. This essay will focus on the failure of leadership evident in the difficulty of the U.S. administration to secure passage of its Emergency Economic Stabilization Act.

On 11 September 2008 the financial markets – and, more important perhaps, the rating agencies – decided that the steps outlined by Chairman Richard Fuld to shore up the balance sheet of the venerable, but embattled, Lehman Brothers would not be enough. The freefall in global equity markets and the freezing of global credit markets began. Over the weekend, Treasury Secretary Henry ('Hank')

Paulson made matters infinitely worse by deciding that the U.S. Treasury would not participate in a way that would permit an orderly takeover of Lehman. Lehman declared bankruptcy – a bankruptcy that is, by a factor of 6, the largest bankruptcy in the history of the world. Unlike 11 September 2001, this crisis moved in slow motion through the weeks that followed as the Treasury had essentially to take over AIG – the world's largest insurance company, make two investment houses into banks, and then, with confidence continuing to crash, construct, and get bipartisan approval from congressional leaders for, a $700-billion rescue package to buy bad debts from ailing banks.

And then something happened. On 29 September, members of the House of Representatives interrupted their personal campaigns for re-election and returned to Washington to shock the world by rejecting the rescue plan. Then they smugly and proudly went back to their constituencies, prepared for the plaudits for 'standing up to Wall Street,' only to see the world's stock markets plunge and their constituents lose over $1 trillion in market value in their mutual funds, pension plans, 401k plans, and the like. A few days later, they returned to Washington again to approve what they had rejected, with a few face-saving amendments and a barrel of favourite goodies added on to induce those final votes.

That fateful week proved to the world that the United States was unable to provide decisive leadership or to take decisive action to deal with the crisis. Over the days and weeks that have passed, more and more piecemeal, occasionally coordinated but more often disjointed, actions have been taken by players around the world. Confidence has not been restored. The global equity markets anticipate worse and worse consequences to come.

We will never know what might have happened if that rescue plan had been passed quickly and uneventfully. We can only speculate on what might have been if the world had seen that the United States was able to act quickly, decisively, and forcefully to events. If the world had seen that the United States had leadership that could bring its own government together and rally its own people, would we have restored some of the confidence that was so quickly regained after that other 9/11? We will never know, but what we can see is that the leadership failures in that crucial month have still not been addressed.

So what went wrong? In my view, we have to see this as a classical failure of leadership. In the intertwining of crisis and leadership, we have witnessed, in dramatic form, what happens when leadership does not happen, when the leader does not step up.

But what is that leaders do? Is it simply a matter of giving great speeches, or of looking confident and making all the right calls? Although we hear, day after day, talk of leadership, and often of leadership failures, how many of us know what leadership is and what it does? In the academic world there has been considerable study of leaders and of the phenomena of leadership. We do know what leaders do and what followers need from leaders. We can break the work of the leader into three groupings of activities: managing, leading, and engaging.

Managing is the hard and necessary work of coming up with concrete solutions to problems and specific ideas for taking advantage of opportunities. It involves creating specific plans with clearly defined steps and milestones to reach. It involves assembling and organizing people to do the work and setting the rules and guidelines for the work. It involves follow-up and control steps to ensure that everything remains on track and that modification to the plan or to the organization takes place as needed to attain the objective.

Leading, to use John Kotter's famous distinction, is a related but distinctly different work. Leading starts with an articulation and communication of a vision of the future, putting into words the purpose of all that managerial action. Leading involves the alignment of a critical mass of people who really believe and understand the vision and the reasons for the specific activity. And leading entails motivating people to take actions that involve significant change to normal routines.

Engaging gets at the deeper motivations that bind us together as humans, that persuades us to come together for the common good and brings out the desire to perform at our best. Engagement begins with the identification of a set of values that underlie specific action. Engagement occurs when there are common goals that we can all aspire to and that demand concerted action to achieve. And engagement happens when we each can find a way to contribute in some small, meaningful, but highly personal way.

If this is what leadership is, what were the leadership failures connected to the financial-rescue package? Again, I will look at these failures under the three headings just set out.

Managing was in evidence but was insufficient. For purposes of this analysis, I will assume that there was nothing fundamentally wrong with the proposal. Indeed, the fact that it was passed a few days later by both the Senate and the House is an indication that, although it had flaws, it was not entirely ill-conceived. Using the leadership framework described above, we can conclude that the administration performed the set of activities that are labelled 'managing.' There was a plan: $700 billion to purchase certain toxic assets. There was an organization, an agency, and a set of defined steps for how that agency would work. And there was a control system in the steps required before certain actions were taken and in the reporting mechanisms.

And so the legislation was presented to Congress as if good management was all that it would take to get approval. But what we know is that we need leadership to make any significant change. We especially need leadership in a time of crisis when we are looking to make sense of what is happening and how we will regain a sense of control in our lives. And we profoundly need leadership when we believe that people and institutions whom we trusted have let us down. And it was leadership that was missing.

Leading was done really badly. Every time the rescue package was labelled a 'bail out,' we could see that leadership was missing. The job of leaders is to articulate and communicate the purpose of an activity in ways that we can understand. If the package is labelled a 'bail out,' its purposes have either not been explained or listeners have not been convinced. The leader's job is to explain and convince. If people are not convinced, the leader has failed.

Engaging was entirely absent. Every time the proposal was described as 'Main Street vs. Wall Street,' we could see that the engaging side of leadership was missing. A leader's job is to demonstrate that proposed actions are consistent with values that the community can rally behind. With the vast majority of Americans far removed from Wall Street, no one would ever vote for a proposal that benefited one elite group over the mainstream public. When people did not see that this was actually an opportunity to rein in Wall Street, to buy assets while they are cheap, to profit from Wall Street excesses, to provide a vehicle that would enable ordinary Americans to take part in saving the American dream and the American way of life, there was a failure of leadership.

The clear and evident fact is that no one explained in a satisfactory way to the American media and, through them, to the American public what had really happened, how the rescue package would really work, and who it was intended to benefit. No one painted a picture of how the United States and the world would perform after the financial system was restored. In fact, it was not until the vote was lost that a few people stepped up to do the leadership job that the so-called 'leaders of the free world' failed to do. It should be embarrassing to elected and appointed leaders that a few non-elected, non-appointed people turned the tide on the rescue package. Suze Orman on CNN made it very plain how the rescue was needed to enable people to continue to use their credit cards. Ali Velshi of CNN drew big charts with very few words to describe how money flows through the system for everyone's benefit. CNN, and likely other parts of the media, performed the essential leadership job of explaining the purpose of the proposal and aligning the necessary coalition of people to make it happen.

Charlie Rose of PBS had Warren Buffett on his program for an hour describing how important it was to use the 'strongest balance sheet' in the world to move funds into the system and making it clear that the rescue package was not a tax on Americans but an investment that could well pay off in a few years. Rose and Buffett performed the essential leadership job of engaging the American people to accept the idea, of enabling them to see that the rescue package was not inconsistent with sound American values. The elected and appointed leadership should take a page from the 'Oracle of Omaha' on what it means to be a leader.

In a few days, the media was educated, opinion leaders understood the idea, and the tone of the public debate changed. Congress voted in favour of the bill and action is gradually being taken – but action that will always be compromised by doubts about the U.S. ability to act quickly and decisively.

If a few people on CNN and PBS provided the leadership, where were the people whom we look to? As in most crises, this failure of leadership is likely a confluence of seemingly unrelated events. Where were the leaders?

The first place we would expect to look would be to the president. President Bush has the problem of being in that uniquely American 'lame duck' position as he completes the few remaining weeks of his term of office. Not only that, he will be leaving the office with the lowest approval rating of any sitting president since such polling began. And, with that low approval rating, he faced a country where many members of his party running for election are doing so on a platform of non-support for the Bush administration.

All that might be enough of an excuse if it were not for the example of Mayor Giuliani, who rallied New Yorkers and all Americans from an equally weak position. The fact is that the president was largely absent in the critical moments. His communications were limited to very brief statements on the White House lawn. There were no visits to homeowners being foreclosed, to small businesses financing the Christmas inventory, to pensioners worrying about their savings. These were the people who needed to know what was happening, to believe that their government was there for them, and to see how they could contribute in some way to protecting and preserving the American dream. It did not happen and to this day it has not happened.

Another figure who could have provided leadership was the secretary of the Treasury, Hank Paulson. Paulson held the position of leadership and had the expertise to understand the system, how it works and how the rescue package was all about the small people not the big people. But, as was true of the president, there were issues that made it difficult for him to lead. He is a public-minded person, but he is not a politician. He is not, as can be seen, a very engaging or convincing public speaker. He looks uncomfortable in front of the camera and in dealing with the press. He carries the public burden of being a wealthy man who cannot pretend to feel the crisis in the way that it will be felt by ordinary Americans. Worse yet, his wealth came from a lifetime on Wall Street where he had access to what most Americans believe to be the excessive compensation and privilege of that part of the economy. For many people, he personifies the problem not the solution. And he was understandably preoccupied with being a manager: planning, organizing, controlling. Finally, he has made it clear that he is not going to stick it out until the situation is solved. Today he admits that the government's plans were poorly communicated, but he has yet to take any responsibility for that failure, or, in fact, even to admit that the administration's poor communication represented a failure at all.

We could go on. Where were our other leaders? Chairman Ben Bernanke of the Federal Reserve has, for some reason, decided to let someone else carry the load of explaining the issue and the way out. Where has the vice-president been? Where were the congressional leaders? Clearly no one wanted to be associated with the mess. Likely few understood it well enough to be leaders of the solution. And no one wants to be associated with the final actions of an unpopular, lame duck president.

Over the past twenty years, crisis management has been extensively studied by scholars like Ian I. Mitroff. We have learned, from the Tylenol crisis to the Bhopal crisis, from the Exxon Valdez crisis to the Enron crisis and, most recently, the Maple Leaf Foods crisis, that there are certain steps that have to be taken. We know how vital visible leadership is. We know that communication is crucial, even when there is nothing to say. In the current financial crisis, it seems that everything we know about crisis leadership has been forgotten. And everything that we know about the failure of effective leadership in crises is being relearned.

Yes, over the past twenty years we have learned a lot about leadership, particularly about its critical role in times of crisis. We now know what it is that leaders have to do. We also have clear and compelling evidence that effective leadership in times of crisis reduces the impact and duration of the crisis and speeds the recovery. There is an equal amount of evidence that ineffective leadership in times of crisis prolongs the situation and can create a condition where the recovery takes years. From that point of view, the failure of leadership in the United States, the centre of the financial crisis, is important and worrisome. It should be no surprise that global stock markets continue to reflect the loss of confidence that investors have in the management of the crisis. Management will never be enough. Leadership and management have to work in tandem.

Nevertheless, there is hope. One of the great features of the American democracy is that every four or eight years the leadership is guaranteed to turn over. In November there will be a new president. Soon thereafter there will be a new secretary of the Treasury. There will be a clean slate. Given the importance of a healthy financial system to our well-being, one can hope that a new slate of people will provide the leadership to accompany all the managerial actions under way, that they will be able to show how the government's actions are consistent with the values that we believe in.

Ultimately, we are a resilient species and we will get through this mess. How quickly we get through it and the place that the United States will play in the leadership of the global economy will be determined in the next few months by the leadership that emerges on 4 November.

2

DERIVATIVES AND RISK MANAGEMENT

The Financial Crisis of 2007:
Another Case of Irrational Exuberance

John Hull

To understand the crisis that has paralysed the world's financial markets since August 2007, it is first necessary to look at the U.S. housing market during the 2000 to 2006 period. This period was characterized by a huge increase in what is termed subprime mortgage lending. Subprime mortgages are mortgages that are considered to be significantly riskier than average. Before 2000, most mortgages classified as subprime were second mortgages. After 2000, this changed as financial institutions became more comfortable with the notion of a subprime first mortgage.

Subprime first mortgages made house purchase possible for many families that had previously not been considered to be sufficiently creditworthy to qualify for a mortgage. These families increased the demand for real estate and prices rose. To mortgage originators, the combination of more lending and higher house prices was attractive. More lending meant bigger profits. Higher house prices meant that the lending was well covered by the underlying collateral. If the borrower defaulted, the house could be repossessed and the lender would not take a loss. Not unnaturally, mortgage originators looked for ways to continue the trend towards more lending and higher house prices.

The problem with higher house prices was that it was difficult to continue to attract new first-time buyers. To overcome this problem, mortgage originators became creative in the way they designed mortgages. The amount lent as a percentage of the house price increased. Adjustable rate mortgages (ARMS) were developed where there was a 'teaser rate' that would last for two or three years. A typical teaser rate was about 6 per cent and the rate after the end of the teaser-rate period was typically six-month London Inter-Bank Offered Interest Rate (LIBOR) plus 6 per cent. (However, teaser rates as low as 1 or 2 per cent have been reported.) Lenders also became more cavalier in the way they reviewed mortgage applications. Indeed, the applicant's income and other information reported on the application were frequently not checked.

A number of terms have been used to describe mortgage lending during the period leading up to the credit crunch. One is 'liar loans' because individuals applying for a mortgage, knowing that no checks would be carried out, sometimes chose to lie on the application form. Another term used to describe some borrowers is *Ninja* (no income, no job, no assets.) To quote A.N. Krinsman: 'In 2005 and 2006 lenders made it easier for borrowers to obtain subprime loans. For example, the typical subprime borrower with a (FICO) credit score between 450 and 680 could obtain a loan with little or no down payment, provide little or no documented proof of income or assets, obtain a loan with a low initial "teaser" interest rate that re-set to a new, higher rate after two or three years.'[1] (Mortgages where the borrower had a FICO score less than 620 were typically classified as subprime, but when the down payment was low, 680 was sometimes used as the subprime cut-off.)

The result of all this was a bubble in house prices. Prices increased very fast during the 2000 to 2006 period and the mortgages granted became progressively riskier. All bubbles burst eventually and this one was no exception. In 2007 many mortgage holders found that they could no longer afford their mortgages when teaser rates ended. This led to foreclosures and large numbers of houses coming on the market, which in turn led to a decline in house prices. Other mortgage holders, who had borrowed 100 per cent, or close to 100 per cent, of the cost of a house found that they had negative equity.

One of the features of the U.S. housing market is that mortgages are non-recourse in many states. This means that, when there is a default, the lender is able to take possession of the house but other assets of the borrower are off-limits. Consequently, the borrower has a free American-style 'put' option. He or she can at any time sell the house to the lender for the principal outstanding on the mortgage. (During the teaser-interest-rate period, the principal typically increased, making this option more valuable.) Lenders realized belatedly how costly the put option could be. If the borrower had negative equity, the optimal decision was to exchange the house for the outstanding principal on the mortgage. The lender then had to sell the house. This process added to the downward pressure on house prices.

It would be a mistake to assume that all mortgage defaulters were in the same position. Some were unable to meet mortgage payments and suffered greatly when they had to give up their homes. But many of the defaulters were speculators who bought multiple homes as rental properties and chose to exercise their put options. It was their tenants who suffered. There are also reports that some house owners (who were not speculators) were quite creative in extracting value from their put options. After handing the keys to their house to the lender, they turned around and bought (sometimes at a bargain price) another house that was in foreclosure. Imagine two people with identical houses next to each other. Both have mortgages of $250,000. Both houses are worth $200,000 and in foreclosure can be expected to sell for $170,000. What is their owners' optimal strategy? The answer is that each person should exercise the put option and buy the neighbour's house. (There were ways of doing this without getting a bad credit rating.)

Figure 2.1
U.S. real estate prices, 1987 to July 2008, S&P/Case-Shiller Composite-10 Index

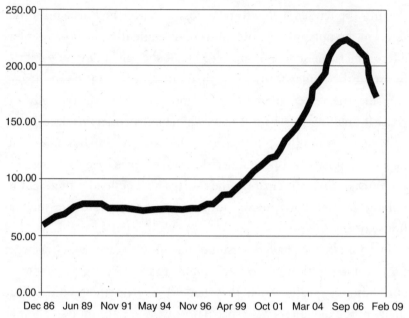

The impact of all of this on house prices in the United States is summarized by Figure 2.1, which shows the S&P/Case-Shiller Composite-10 Index for house prices between January 1987 and July 2008. During the 2000 to 2006 period, house prices increased much faster than they had in previous years. In 2007, when the bubble burst, prices showed steep declines.

The United States was not alone in seeing lending practices relaxed. This also happened in the United Kingdom. One feature of the U.K. market was mortgages (and remortgages) of 120 per cent of the purchase price. Luckily, the mortgage market was more sane in Canada. Here, 100 per cent mortgages were not possible for most of the 2000 to 2007 period. Mortgages with down payments between 5 per cent and 20 per cent of the purchase price could be arranged, but mortgage insurance (paid for by the borrower) had to be obtained.

ABSs and ABS CDOs

The originators of mortgages in the United States did not in many instances keep the mortgages themselves. They sold the mortgages to companies that created structured products from them. This helps to explain why they relaxed their lending standards. When lenders considered new mortgage applications, the question was not 'Is this a credit we want to assume?' Instead it was 'Is this a mortgage we can make money on by selling it to someone else?'

The simplest structured product that was created was an ABS (asset-backed security). This is illustrated in Figure 2.2. A portfolio of assets (such as subprime mortgages) is created and the cash flows from the mortgages are allocated to tranches. In Figure 2.2 there are three tranches. These are the senior tranche, the mezzanine tranche, and the equity tranche. (This is a simplification of reality. In practice there are usually about six tranches.) The portfolio has a principal of $100 million. This is divided as follows: $75 million to the senior tranche, $20 million to the mezzanine tranche, and $5 million to the equity tranche. The senior tranche is promised a return of 6 per cent, the mezzanine tranche is promised a return of 10 per cent, and the equity tranche is promised a return of 30 per cent.

It sounds as though the equity tranche has the best deal, but this is not necessarily the case. The equity tranche is much less likely to realize its return than the other two tranches. Cash flows are allocat-

Figure 2.2
An asset-backed security (simplified)

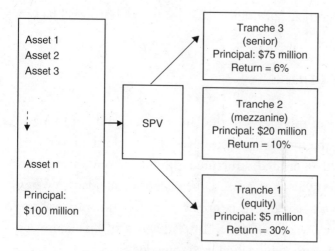

ed to tranches by specifying what is known as a waterfall. The general way a waterfall works is illustrated in Figure 2.3. The cash flows from the assets are allocated to the senior tranche until the senior tranche has received its promised return. Assuming that the promised return to the senior tranche can be made, cash flows are then allocated to the mezzanine tranche. If the promised return to the mezzanine tranche can be made and cash flows are left over, they are allocated to the equity tranche. The precise waterfall rules were generally outlined in a legal document several hundred pages long.

The structure in Figure 2.2 typically lasts several years. At the end, principal payments are distributed to tranches. The extent to which the tranches get their principal back depends on losses on the assets. The first 5 per cent of losses are borne by the equity tranche. If losses exceed 5 per cent, the equity tranche loses all its principal and some losses are borne by the mezzanine tranche. If losses exceed

Figure 2.3
The waterfall

Asset
cash
flows

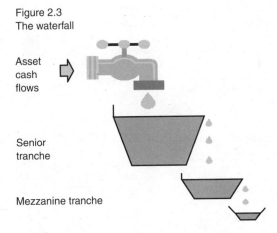

Senior
tranche

Mezzanine tranche

25 per cent, the mezzanine loses all its principal and some losses are borne by the senior tranche.

There are therefore two ways of looking at an ABS. One is with reference to the waterfall in Figure 2.3. Cash flows go first to the senior tranche, then to the mezzanine tranche, and then to the equity tranche. The other is in terms of losses. Losses of principal are first borne by the equity tranche, then by the mezzanine tranche, and then by the senior tranche.

The ABS is designed so that the senior tranche is rated AAA. The mezzanine tranche is typically rated BBB. The equity tranche is usually unrated. Finding investors to buy AAA-rated tranches is not difficult. The equity tranche is typically retained by the originator of the assets or sold to a hedge fund. However, finding investors for the mezzanine tranche is not easy. This led financial engineers to be creative (arguably too creative). Financial engineers devised an ABS from the mezzanine tranches of ABSs that were created from subprime mortgages. This is known as an ABS CDO (Collaterized Debt Obligation) and is illustrated in Figure 2.4.

Figure 2.4
An ABS CDO (simplified)

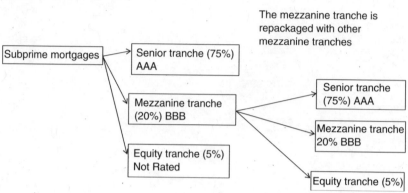

The senior tranche of the ABS CDO is rated AAA. This means that the total of the AAA-rated instruments created in the example that is considered here is 90 per cent (75 per cent plus 75 per cent of 20 per cent) of the principal of the underlying mortgage portfolio. This seems high, but, if the securitization were carried further with an ABS being created from the mezzanine tranches of ABS CDOs (and this did happen), the percentage would be pushed even higher.

In my example (admittedly simplified), the AAA-rated tranche of the ABS in Figure 2.2 would probably have been downgraded in the second half of 2007. However, it will receive the promised return if losses on the underlying mortgage portfolio are less than 25 per cent because all losses of principal are absorbed by the more junior tranches. The AAA-rated tranche of the ABS CDO in Figure 2.4 is much riskier. It will get paid the promised return if losses on the underlying portfolio are 10 per cent or less because in that case mezzanine tranches of ABSs have to absorb losses equal to at most 5 per cent of the ABS principal. Since they have a total principal of 20 per

Table 2.1
Losses to AAA tranches of ABS CDO in example

Losses to subprime portfolios	Losses to mezzanine tranche of ABS	Losses to equity tranche of ABS CDO	Losses to mezzanine tranche of ABS CDO	Losses to senior tranche of ABS CDO
10%	25%	100%	100%	0%
15%	50%	100%	100%	33.3%
20%	75%	100%	100%	66.7%
25%	100%	100%	100%	100%

cent of the ABS principal, their loss is at most 5/20 or 25 per cent. This wipes out the equity and mezzanine tranches of the ABS CDO but leaves the senior tranche unscathed. The senior tranche of the ABS CDO does suffer losses if losses on the underlying portfolios are more than 10 per cent. Consider, for example, the situation where losses are 20 per cent on the underlying portfolios. In this case, losses on the mezzanine tranches are 15/20 or 75 per cent of their principal. The first 25 per cent is absorbed by the equity and mezzanine tranches of the ABS CDO. The senior tranche of the ABS CDO therefore loses 50/75 or 66.7 per cent of its value. These and other results are summarized in Table 2.1.

The valuations of the tranches of ABSs and (especially) ABS CDOs are heavily dependent on default correlation. If mortgages default independently of each other, or with very little correlation (as they do in normal times), the risk associated with senior tranches is small. But, if default correlation is high (as it is in stressed market conditions), the risk is much higher.

Many banks have lost money investing in the senior tranches of ABS CDOs. The investments were typically financed at LIBOR and promised a return quite a bit higher than LIBOR. Because they were rated AAA, the capital requirements were minimal. Merrill Lynch is an example of a bank that lost a great deal of money from investments in ABS CDOs. In July 2008 Merrill Lynch agreed to sell senior tranches of ABS CDOs that had previously been rated AAA and had a principal of $30.6 billion to Lone Star Funds for twenty-two cents on the dollar.[2]

Avoiding Future Crises

Many factors contributed to the financial crisis. Mortgage originators used lax lending standards. Products were developed to enable mortgage originators to profitably transfer credit risk to investors. The products bought by investors were complex and in many instances investors and rating agencies had inaccurate or incomplete information about the quality of the underlying assets. Rating agencies moved from their traditional business of rating loans to rating structured products and assigned an AAA rating to tranches that were in some cases highly dependent on the default correlation between the underlying assets. Investors in the structured products that were created thought they had found a money machine and chose to rely on rating agencies rather than forming their own opinions about the underlying risks.

How can future crises be avoided? Here are a few observations:

1. The present crisis might have been less severe if the originators of mortgages and other assets that were securitized were required by regulators to keep, say, 20 per cent of each tranche that was created. This would have better aligned the interests of origina-

tors with the interests of the investors who bought the products. The market for structured products has now virtually disappeared. However, the finance sector has a short memory. The market will reappear at some future time. Regulators and rating agencies should be sensitive to situations where the interests of parties are not aligned.

2. There should be less emphasis on short-term compensation in financial institutions. At present, many employees at all level of seniority in financial institutions receive much of their compensation in the form of annual bonuses. This reflects performance over a twelve-month period. Imagine you are an employee of a financial institution investing in ABS CDOs in 2006. Almost certainly you would have recognized that there was a bubble in the U.S. housing market and would expect that bubble to burst sooner or later. However, it is possible that you would decide to continue with your ABS CDO investments. If the bubble did not burst until after 31 December 2006, you would still get a nice bonus at the end of 2006. In another work I suggest one way in which bonuses can reflect performance over a longer time period than one year.[3]

3. Financial institutions should construct their own models to assess the risk in the products they buy. It appears that many financial institutions did not do this for ABS CDOs. This is surprising because an ABS CDO is a very complex product. It is similar to what is called a CDO squared in the synthetic CDO market. CDO squareds are recognized by traders as highly risky products that are difficult to price. The market for them disappeared largely for this reason a few years ago. A tranche of an ABS CDO is no less risky and no less difficult to price than a

CDO squared, but it was nevertheless considered by many financial institutions to be a good investment. Because models were not developed, the key role of default correlation in valuing ABS CDOs was not well understood by some investors.

4. It is important that risk management involve both models and human judgment. A risk-management committee should meet regularly to consider the key risks facing a financial institution. Stress tests should be based on the scenarios generated by these managers in addition to those generated from historical data. The risk-management committee should be particularly sensitive to situations where high profits are being made without any special skills being used and without any risks being identified. One of the lessons from past financial crises is that correlations increase in stressed market conditions. Using standard techniques to estimate correlations from past data and assuming that those correlations will apply in stressed markets is not appropriate. One of the roles of the risk-management committee during the period leading up to the crisis would have been to recognize the bubble in house prices and insist that stress tests be carried out to examine the impact of rising default rates in all parts of the country. Of course, it is also important that the senior bank management actually listen to their risk managers and other advisers. There is some evidence that they are reluctant to do this during good times.[4]

Conclusion

Irrational exuberance was a term coined by Alan Greenspan during the bull market of the 1990s. Both mortgage originators and mortgage investors showed a large amount of irrational exuberance during the period leading up to August 2007. They thought that the 'good times' would last forever and, because compensation plans focused their attention on short-term profits, they chose to ignore the risks they were taking.

We are all now paying the price.

NOTES

1 A.N. Krinsman, 'Subprime Mortgage Meltdown: How Did It Happen and How Will It End?' *Journal of Structured Finance* (summer 2007): 13–19.
2 In fact, the deal was worse than it sounds for Merrill Lynch because Merrill Lynch agreed to finance 75 per cent of the purchase price. If the value of the ABS CDO tranches went down below 16.5 cents on the dollar, Merrill Lynch might find itself owning the assets again.
3 J.C. Hull, 'The Credit Crunch of 2007: What Went Wrong? Why? What Lessons Can Be Learned?' International Proceedings Volume of Conference Sponsored by Chicago Federal Reserve Board and European Central Bank, September 2008.
4 Some bank employees such as Keishi Hotsuki, co-head of risk management at Merrill Lynch, and David Rosenberg, chief North American economist at Merrill Lynch, did sound warning bells ahead of the credit crunch, but were ignored. Ed Clark, CEO at TD Bank, who had the foresight to close down the bank's structured-products business ahead of the crisis, has indicated that this decision met with huge opposition within the bank.

3

STRUCTURED FINANCE

Subprime, Market Meltdown, and Learning from the Past

Laurence Booth

I believe that banking institutions are more dangerous to our liberties than standing armies.

– Thomas Jefferson[1]

The Problem

This quotation from Thomas Jefferson has received a lot of play in the last month and rightly so, for, now as in Jefferson's day, the implications of a fractional reserve system on credit creation and destruction are of paramount importance. Over the last year we have seen the following institutions fail, be taken over, or be effectively brought under state control: Fannie Mae, Freddie Mac, Washington Mutual, Wachovia, Bear Stearns, Lehman Brothers, Merrill Lynch, American International Group (AIG), and National City in the United States; Bradford and Bingley, Northern Rock, and HBOS in the United Kingdom; Fortis in Belgium, the Netherlands, and Luxembourg; and Hypo Real Estate Holdings in Germany.

Not only banking institutions have failed. Iceland had to seek a $6-billion bailout from Russia, Ireland had to guarantee all its bank deposits, and Ukraine had to seek a $16.5-billion emergency loan from the International Monetary Fund (IMF). And the fallout is not over yet. U.S. hedge funds and investors are massively repatriating cash to the United States to meet margin calls and redemptions,[2] leading to huge drops in international stock markets and an appreciating U.S. dollar. In response, Hungary has sought emergency funding from the IMF. South Korea, on 27 October 2008, slashed its central bank rate by 0.75 per cent for only the second time in history and its president announced massive new spending plans to lift the economy. In Japan the Nikkei Index dropped to the level of twenty-six years ago, while the Yen continued to appreciate as investors had to sell foreign investments to pay back Japanese loans and unwind the 'carry trade.'[3] Russia, in contrast, simply closed its markets as the Russian stock market lost 75 per cent of its value! And Canada? With the collapse in the price of oil per barrel from a high of $147 to barely $60, the loonie has fallen from parity to $US0.77 in less than a month, while the TSX Composite is off 40–45 per cent from its summer highs.

At the moment, the cost of this disaster is anybody's guess. So far, U.S. banks have written off over $500 billion and destroyed much of their bank capital in the process, to the extent that a Republican government has had to put together a $700-billion bailout plan and inject $250 billion directly into the banks by buying bank preferred shares. The United Kingdom has injected $63 billion into three of its banks and effectively nationalized Bradford and Bingley and Northern Rock, two large mortgage lenders, while the major bank regulator in Germany has indicated that the collapse of the U.S. investment bank Lehman Brothers has cost European banks at least $300 billion.

However, the real cost has been reflected in the massive destruction of wealth in the stock market. The U.S. Congressional Budget Office has indicated that U.S. retirement accounts had lost over $2 trillion by the end of September, and since then the U.S. market has lost another 20 per cent plus so the loss must now be over $3 trillion. The California Public Employee Retirement System (Calpers) alone has seen the value of its assets drop from around $250 billion to $192 billion in a year and is considering requiring increased employer contribution rates of 2–4 per cent of payroll. What this does to the retirement plans of Americans is unclear, except that the number of years people must work is bound to increase.

The reason for the losses is not hard to find. Table 3.1 gives the losses in U.S. dollars for the year to date for the eight major equity markets in the world.[4] As of the end of 2006, the total market value was about US$36 trillion. Without counting any increased market values for 2007, so far in 2008 the losses are about US$14 trillion, excluding the bigger percentage losses in emerging markets. It is a reasonable question to ask how on earth this happened.

The Cause

To understand the root cause of the problem we have first to recognize that the banking system operates on a fractional reserve system. This means that only a small part of the deposits in a bank are backed by cash and liquid marketable securities, the rest being loaned out to individuals on anything from short to medium terms. If the reserves are 10 per cent, it means that for every dollar of reserves a bank will have a deposit liability of $10, with the $9 difference loaned out or invested in marketable securities. The result is that no bank, however stable and well run, can meet the demands of depositors should they all want their money back immediately. Banks therefore keep prudent reserves to meet unexpected liquidity shocks and have access to the central bank 'discount window' for emergency funding.[5] It is also why they have deposit insurance, so that small investors do not have to worry about getting their money back.

The Bank for International Settlements (BIS) has set standards to ensure that banks do not engage in aggressive lending. This requires that every on-balance sheet loan and off-balance sheet commitment

Table 3.1
Equity-market losses, 2008

Index or exchange	Last trade date	1 day change	1 day %	1 month %	6 month %	YTD %	2006 $b value
United States composite (US$)	213.40 10/24/2008	−7.52	−3.40%	−27.53%	−37.17%	−40.46%	18,039
Japan composite (US$)	82.39 10/24/2008	−2.74	−3.21%	−22.00%	−32.07%	−35.54%	4,422
United Kingdom composite (US$)	149.79 10/24/2008	−11.63	−7.21%	−35.44%	−48.66%	−52.51%	3,441
Canada composite (US$)	278.25 10/24/2008	−4.74	−1.67%	−40.46%	−48.15%	−49.61%	1,636
Germany composite (US$)	218.89 10/24/2008	−14.62	−6.26%	−39.40%	−51.88%	−56.28%	1,426
Hong Kong composite (US$)	186.44 10/24/2008	−10.10	−5.14%	−31.80%	−51.39%	−57.97%	1,361
Spain composite (US$)	388.93 10/24/2008	−26.01	−6.27%	−34.22%	−50.24%	−51.93%	1,146
Switzerland composite (US$)	374.65 10/24/2008	−10.44	−2.71%	−22.21%	−32.06%	−34.35%	1,111

be risk weighted and that a bank have 8 per cent of its risk-weighted loans as capital. In this way a loan to the government does not require the same amount of capital to support it as a loan to a corporation. Of the 8 per cent risk-weighted capital, a minimum of 4 per cent must be common equity-like securities (Tier 1) and the balance (Tier 2) be in subordinated debt and preferred shares. However, while Canada has adopted these requirements, the Office of the Superintendent of Financial Institutions (OSFI) requires the Canadian banks to have 7 per cent Tier 1 capital and another 3 per cent in Tier 2 capital. This means that Canada has one of the most conservative capital standards anywhere in the world. Further, the Canadian banks exceed the OSFI requirements; the Royal Bank of Canada, for example, routinely has almost 12 per cent total capital. In contrast, United States and United Kingdom banks have operated with much less Tier 1 capital, since the BIS guidelines call for only a minimum of 4 per cent in common equity-like securities. In good times, operating with less equity-like capital increases the bank's financial leverage and enhances the return to the shareholder and the bank's stock price. However, in bad times, a bank's higher leverage comes back to bite it.

The use of leverage by the banks brings us to the subprime problem that started the current crisis. It is axiomatic that bad loans are made at the top of the business cycle, not the bottom. At the top of the business cycle, the financial system is flush with liquidity and demand by borrowers tends to drop off. As a result, there is intense pressure on the banks to loan out money on narrower and narrower spreads over risk-free government bonds. As a result, lending standards slip. Everyone 'knows' that this happens; the problem is that no one knows which are the bad loans! In the early 2000s, the bad loans were to quasi-utility companies like Enron and Worldcomm, which were inventing a new deregulated utility paradigm around the Internet and energy trading. In fact, of course, these loans simply created the biggest U.S. corporate bankruptcies to that time.

Bankers always claim that they have learned their lesson and that this time it will be different. However, the liquidity in the financial system through 2006 was enormous. By January 2007, new issues of non-investment-grade debt[6] were running at $127 billion a year, twice the level of 2002. *Business Week* attributed this to the 'enormous amount of money sloshing around and the changing structure of the debt market. Foreign investors are shipping gobs of cash into the US.' The journal concluded: 'Together these factors have combined to create unheard of pools of liquidity. Not only has that helped keep the lid on interest rates – holding debt payments down – it has also made funding readily available even for struggling companies.'[7]

The large pools of liquidity were in part coming from the enormous trade deficits run by the United States and the fact that the United States would not allow China, in particular, to buy real assets or U.S. companies. China had been let into the world's trading club and had a rapidly increasing trade surplus with the United States, but by default it was reinvesting its surplus foreign-exchange reserves in U.S. government and agency debt, mainly the mortgage debt issued by Fannie and Freddie.[8]

The U.S. mortgage market is the key to understanding this crisis. In 1999 the New York *Times* reported that the Clinton administration was pressuring Fannie Mae to ease lending standards to make more mortgage money available to low- and middle-income borrowers.[9] At the time, Peter Wallison of the American Enterprise In-

Figure 3.1
U.S. house prices, Case-Shiller Index

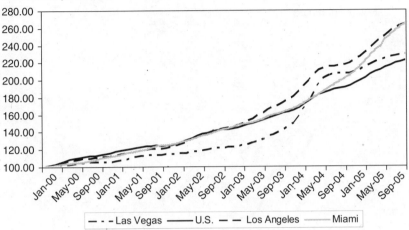

stitute presciently remarked: 'From the perspective of many people, including me, this is another thrift industry growing up around us ... If they fail, the government will have to step up and bail them out the way it stepped up and bailed out the thrift industry.'

When President Bush took office, his administration continued the policy of encouraging home ownership.[10] Several U.S. states tried to rein in aggressive bank lending, which they regarded as 'predatory.' But in each case the office of the Controller of the Currency, which regulates U.S. banks, persuaded the courts to overrule the states on the basis that it was important to have one national standard for banks. In practice, this meant that it was almost a race to the bottom in terms of regulatory standards.

For a time, the reduction in underwriting and credit standards was not noticeable since house prices were rising rapidly, partly because of the very low interest rate policy adopted by the U.S. Federal

Figure 3.2
Credit standards for non-financial firms

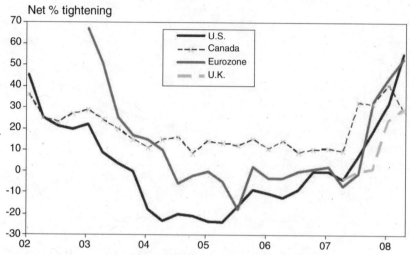

Source: U.S. Senior Loan Officer Survey, ECB Bank Leading Survey, BOE Credit Conditions Survey, BOC Business Outlook Survey, RBC Economics Research. Compiled by RBC Economics.

Reserve Board to pull the United States out of the recession of the early 2000s. Figure 3.1 is the Case-Shiller Index of U.S. house prices for the overall United States, Los Angeles, Miami, and Las Vegas from 2000 to 2006. It was difficult to see much risk when you lent money to buy a house in Los Angeles or Miami, where the average prices had increased from an index value of 100 in January 2000 to 250 six years later. Even a 125 per cent mortgage was quickly pared down to 50 per cent in such hot markets. To many it seemed an easy way to make money and there was so much money floating around that credit standards were getting more relaxed all the time.

Figure 3.2[11] shows just how lax credit standards in most markets had become. However, note that the change was much greater in the United States than in Canada. Whereas household indebtedness as a percentage of net worth was reasonably constant at 21 per cent in Canada, in the United States it increased dramatically from 16 per cent in 2000 to 25 per cent by 2008.

The Leverage

The increased indebtedness of U.S. households was partly a result of financial innovation. The United States has always had a very strange financial system. Unlike most countries, there have been severe restrictions on banks branching outside their state and sometimes even within their state. Further, because interest-rate restrictions made it impossible for banks to offer competitive deposit rates, there was huge *disintermediation* as money flowed to money market mutual funds, rather than through the banking system as happens in Canada. As a result, several powerful investment banks, like Lehman Brothers, Goldman Sachs, and Merrill Lynch, played a much more important role in the U.S. financial system than their counterparts, like Dominion Securities and Wood Gundy, ever did in Canada. Moreover, this was even before the Canadian dealers were taken over by the Canadian chartered banks. More important, these U.S. investment banks recycled the money back to the banks, making U.S. banks much more exposed to the money market than their Canadian equivalents. Unlike the Canadian banks, with a large and captive deposit base, many U.S. banks were dependent on access to the financial market for funding.

The final link in the puzzle was the development of securitization vehicles. Because of the fractured nature of the U.S. banking system, with thousands of local banks, each bank was more exposed to local risks than their Canadian equivalents, which branched right across the country and thus achieved geographic diversification. In order to solve this problem of increased risk, U.S. banks packaged their loans into special investment vehicles (SIVs). At first, these SIVs were traded among individual banks to allow them to diversify their risk. Increasingly, however, they were sold to major investors hungry for yield in a world full of liquidity. It was a simple step to use these SIVs to package residential mortgages for resale to large investors, thereby making these mortgages more and more risky.

The securitizing of the U.S. residential mortgage market was helped by technological developments that allowed the banks to outsource almost the whole process. FICO credit scores were used to judge the creditworthiness of the applicant, even though a cottage industry developed to counsel people on how to get better FICO scores. Mortgage brokers were used to generate the mortgages, even though in some cases they seemed to be in league with developers who were growing increasingly restive at the slowing pace of house sales. Even the routine check on the house value and the income of the applicant was outsourced or not done at all, resulting in the so-called *Ninja* loans: no income, no job, no assets!

Ridiculous as it now seems, Goldman Sachs was able to package a portfolio of 8,274 California second mortgages worth $494 million for resale to sophisticated institutional investors in the spring of 2006.[12] The issue (GSAMP Trust 2006-S3) was one of 916 such issues in 2006 for a total of $592 billion. The average mortgage was for 99.29 per cent of the appraised house value, so the equity was 0.71 per cent – and, no, that is not a typo! Further, 58 per cent of the mortgages had no or little documentation and many had low or 'teaser' rates to entice people into the house purchase. The remarkable thing is that Goldman was able to structure these mortgages such that 93 per cent of the securities issued against them were rated investment grade. As a result, they were easily sold to large institutions looking for increased yield over U.S. Treasuries in a world flush with liquidity. More important, no financial institution took responsibility for the process and U.S. states that tried to impose such liability, like Georgia, were shot down in court.

These SIVs were carefully analysed to spread the risk, but the basic assumption was that, based on historical statistics, the default rate would be only 1.0 per cent. Further, the spread between the expected interest from these subprime mortgages and the interest expense on the mortgage-backed securities of 2.85 per cent was the cushion designed to offset any increase in defaults. Of course, 'the best laid plans of mice and men ...' By the spring of 2007, the default rate had jumped to 18 per cent and that was before things really started to crater. The unfortunate fact is that historical statistics don't matter in a world where house prices are in a bubble and growth is unsustainable!

Figure 3.3 shows the Case-Shiller Index from January 2006 until the present. U.S. house prices peaked in January 2007, with Miami at an index value of 270; since then it has been downhill all the way, and by the late summer of this year the index values were in the 150 to 200 level. In Miami the index stood at 180, meaning that a $270,000 condo had lost a third of its value. Not just subprime but also regular first mortgages were under water. Across the United States as a whole, house prices dropped by 16.3 per cent for the year ending August 2008, enough to wipe out a very large part of the subprime mortgage market, which was about 11 per cent of the U.S. mortgage market as a whole. On top of the subprime mess, a large number of mortgages with low interest or teaser rates were also com-

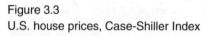

Figure 3.3
U.S. house prices, Case-Shiller Index

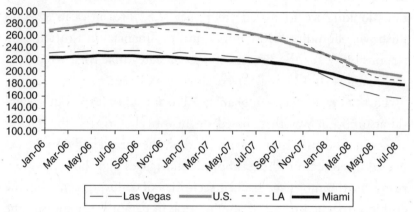

ing up for reset to market rates. The result has been a devastating decline in U.S. house construction, with single-family housing permits down 41 per cent year over year by August 2008.

In the face of this storm of defaults, it is little wonder that U.S. banks have started writing off large numbers of subprime mortgages and taking huge hits to their capital. With the decline in bank capital came concerns about bank solvency, particularly for institutions like Washington Mutual, Citibank, National City, Wachovia, and Merrill Lynch, with their heavy exposure to subprime. It was in this atmosphere that bank runs started: not from retail deposits covered by insurance but from large institutions with no such coverage. First, Bear Stearns faced such a run and was 'rescued' in March 2008 by a forced sale to J.P Morgan Chase at a knock-down price. However, when Lehman Brothers faced a similar run, the U.S. Treasury secretary refused to bail it out and Lehman went into bankruptcy. Shortly after, the government took ownership of AIG, believing that, if it did not, the company's web of insurance contracts might

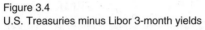

Figure 3.4
U.S. Treasuries minus Libor 3-month yields

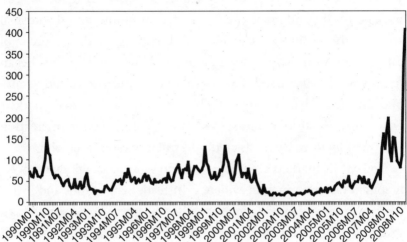

bring down the whole financial system. AIG had guaranteed many of the subprime debt issues for the major banks and as this insurance was 'called' AIG became insolvent. Unlike the case of Lehman Brothers, the U.S. Treasury secretary feared that a failure of AIG would cause spillover effects at many of the major banks, including Goldman Sachs and Citibank.

The Consequences

The effects were immediate: if the U.S. government wouldn't help Lehman and Washington Mutual, then who would it help? The result was a collapse in confidence as banks hoarded cash in case they faced similar runs to that which brought down Lehman and Wash-Mu.[13] Quite simply, banks stopped lending to each other and lent only to their very best customers. Figure 3.4 is the yield on the three-month London Inter-Bank Offered Interest Rate (LIBOR) and the yield on U.S. 90 Treasury Bills. Usually, this spread is about 50–100 basis points depending on credit-market conditions and the normal stage of the business cycle. However, starting in the summer of 2007, the subprime mess became more obvious and spreads began to increase. By October 2008, as banks became afraid to lend to anyone, this spread ballooned to 400 basis points and the credit markets were frozen. Instead, banks started calling loans, and credit creation went rapidly into reverse as credit destruction or deleveraging.

Today, the markets are still frozen and signs of thawing are eagerly sought but not much in evidence. Instead, hedge funds and investors are massively moving to cash either for portfolio reasons or as a result of margin calls and investors demanding their money back. It is an unfortunate fact that, while confidence is easily destroyed by bad policy decisions, it is difficult to get it back. The result is that it seems that every time the U.S. government makes an announcement the stock market drops 500 points and it is left to others, like the left-leaning French president and current president of the European Union, Nicolas Sarkozy, to claim the high ground through decisive action.

The truth is that you cannot make banks lend or individuals borrow even if you shore up bank capital. While the US$700-billion rescue package has earmarked $250 billion for capital infusions into the banking system, there is still no certainty as to who will get the funds and who will not. This uncertainty is being resolved as the funds are allocated, but the process is taking time and in the interval the stock market has collapsed as the freeze in bank lending and the associated credit crunch signals that a severe recession is inevitable. Whether we are in a Keynesian liquidity trap, where monetary poli-

cy will not work, is too early to tell, but, intriguingly, the chairman
of the Federal Reserve Board, Ben Bernanke, has stated before Congress that fiscal stimulus is now needed in the United States. In years
gone by, we would have said that we needed some good old fash-
ioned 'Keynesian pump priming.'

The Future

So where do we go from here? One thing is sure: there is a greater
awareness of the problems facing us now than in 1930, so talk of a
repeat of the Great Depression is alarmist and unlikely. We have relearned the lessons that our great-grandparents learned the hard way
– that banking is special and banks need to be very carefully regulated. Otherwise, credit creation, when it goes into reverse as credit destruction or deleveraging, is a harrowing experience. We have also
learned that Canada got it right and the United States wrong. Banks
need more capital than the BIS requires as a minimum and this
needs to be Tier 1 or common equity capital. Further, banks need a
captive deposit base and so the market solution engineered in the
United States to solve the unique problems of its financial system is
not optimal.

Interestingly, one of the few things that the U.S. secretary of the
Treasury has got right is that the U.S. banking system needs to be
consolidated – and fast. Bank America buying Merrill Lynch, Wells
Fargo buying Wachovia, and J.P Morgan buying Washington Mutual are simply the first steps in the emergence of a U.S. financial
system that will mirror Canada's, with hegemonic banks branching
coast to coast. It is the nightmare that populist U.S. politicians, like
Thomas Jefferson, have feared for two hundred years and will result

in behemoths that are simply too big to fail, but then Lehman brothers was as well!

We must bring back things that were deregulated away in the United States: people need a down payment for a house; the value of the house needs to be appraised; incomes need to be checked; and, finally, the value of credit restrictions needs to be recognized. Perhaps it makes sense that people pay down their mortgage on a monthly basis, instead of having negative amortization mortgage, a teaser low interest rate, and a prayer that their incomes will rise to offset the higher future payments.

The U.S. secretary of the Treasury, Henry Paulson, said on the Fox Business Network (16 October 2008): 'We're not proud of all the mistakes that were made by many different people, different parties, failures of our regulatory system, failures of market discipline that got us here.' What is remarkable, however, is that true leaders know that leadership starts from and ends at the top. Paulson's laying the blame on a wide range of parties, rather than his own department and himself, is quite amazing. Former U.S. President Harry Truman had the sense to acknowledge that 'the buck stops here.' George Bush and Henry Paulson will go down as the leaders who 'broke the buck.'[14]

NOTES

1 The Debate over the Re-charter of The Bank Bill (1809).
2 When purchases are partly made with borrowed money (margin), the lender can demand that more cash be invested if the shares drop in value.
3 The carry trade consisted of borrowing in low-interest-rate countries like Japan and investing in higher interest-rate countries.

4   Yahoo Finance, http://investing.businessweek.com/research/markets/world/worldmarkets.asp?region=Americas.

5   The Bank of Canada has an emergency lending facility (ELF) for Canadian banks. Funds are lent if there is a liquidity shock and the Office of the Superintendent of Financial Institutions believes that the institution is sound.

6   Non-investment-grade is debt rated below BBB and generally faces a more restricted market than investment-grade debt.

7   29 January 2007.

8   There is at least a suspicion that this is why the U.S. government guaranteed the debt of these institutions, while throwing the equity and preferred shareholders to the wolves.

9   'Fannie Mae Eases Credit to Aid Mortgage Lending,' 30 September 1999.

10 Unlike in Canada, U.S. mortgage interest, for example, remains tax-deductible.

11 *RBC Economics,* 'Economic and Financial Market Outlook,' October 2008.

12 Alan Sloan, 'House of Junk,' *Fortune,* 29 October 2007.

13 WashMu had $18 billion in cash but lost $16 billion in forty-eight hours after the U.S. House of Representatives refused at first to pass the bail-out bill and it was downgraded by Standard and Poors and taken over by the Federal Deposit Insurance Corporation.

14 This is an in-joke. U.S. money market funds are regulated so that the par value is $1. With the Lehman loss, most funds dropped below $1 (broke the buck) and faced massive redemptions until the U.S. government stepped in to guarantee them all.

4

VALUE INVESTING

Value Investing in the Crisis: How Margins of Safety Melted Away

Eric Kirzner

The current financial crisis is now in its seventeenth month. News about massive mortgage defaults and concerns about the viability of certain mortgage and investment banks began to appear in the media around May 2007. The stock market went pretty well sideways for the next year, actually hitting a new high in May 2008. However, the bad news accelerated in the summer of 2008, resulting in a market meltdown which started in July and August 2008 as a ripple and then accelerated to a firestorm in September and early October. From 28 August to 10 October 2008, Toronto's S&P/ TSX Composite Index lost 34.2 per cent, while the U.S S&P500 and the Dow Jones Industrial Averages[1] lost 30.8 per cent and 28.9 per cent respectively.[2] The global scene was just as bad, with the Morgan Stanley Capital International EAFE Index[3] losing 33.2 per cent over the same period.

You have to go back to the Great Crash to find a comparable period.[4] The Dow, from its high on 3 September 1929 to its near term low on 13 November 1929, fell by 48 per cent. By 8 July 1932 it was down by 89.4 per cent!

Although the crisis became visible in 2007, the seeds of the market meltdown were sown in the early 2000s. Against a period of rising housing prices and low interest rates, home mortgages were offered (with specialized terms) to subprime borrowers who were sold on the notion that they too could live the 'The American Dream' and participate in a housing market they previously thought was out of their reach. Many of the mortgage loans were 'teasers' with artificially low interest rates (such as 1 per cent or 2 per cent) for the first two or three years and often no principal repayment requirements or even in some cases negative amortization.[5] Some of the loans were so-called Liar Loans which allowed borrowers simply to state their income – the statements were not subject to verification. Meanwhile, these very low-quality loans were sold by mortgage banks to investment banks where they were bundled into packages of assets and liabilities called Mortgage Backed Securities and Collateralized Debt Obligations. Against this background, stock market prices were rising steadily. Global markets started to rally just days before President Bush's 19 March 2003 'Moment of Truth' and the ensuing launch of the Iraq War. As it turned out, some of this rally was based on illusory assumptions about the real state of the financial system.

As housing prices started to slow and then fall around July 2006, many of the teaser loans reached their reset period and borrowers were faced with payment shocks as monthly mortgage payments often quintupled or more. There were considerable defaults as homeowners, looking at negative equity in their homes, walked away from their houses and mortgages.[6] As default rates increased, Wall Street investment banks examined loan details on delinquent files and put them back to mortgage banks. There was a massive miscalculation of the propensity of borrowers to default when loan-to-value ratios exceed 100 per cent.[7] And so a lethal combination of greed, misrepresentation, and stupidity created a financial disaster.

The Value Investing Approach

So you can see the steps leading to the current crisis. How did the venerable value approach to investing made famous by Benjamin Graham and his noted disciples such as Warren Buffett and Sir John Templeton fare during this period? Not at all well. However, if you understand the value world, you will see why! Let me first take you through the world of value investing and then we will look at its performance during the crisis.

Value investing is associated with a number of investment legends. The founder was Benjamin Graham, whose 1934 book *Security Analysis,* with co-author David Dodd, is still considered the genesis of modern security analysis. Graham was a Columbia University graduate who worked on Wall Street. In 1928 he taught a course on security analysis at Columbia where he set out some of the foundations of his approach. Later, as a student of the Great Crash, Graham argued that security analysis should be a number-crunching quantitative approach, using techniques that could be universally applied and available from publicly available sources. His approach focused on price-to-earnings ratios (P/Es), price-to-book ratios (P/Bs), debt-to-equity ratios, dividend records, net current assets, and earnings growth. Graham liked to look for unpopular or neglected companies with low P/E and P/B ratios. He also analysed financial statements and footnotes to understand whether companies have hidden assets (e.g., investments in other companies) that are potentially unnoticed by the market. Graham believed that you could estimate a stock's intrinsic value by estimating the value of a company's net assets, analysing its current earnings, and forecasting its future earnings. Those who studied under Graham at Columbia were Warren Buffett and Sir John Templeton.

Warren Buffett is arguably the world's most famous value investor. His approach of finding great companies, buying them at bargain prices, and holding them 'forever' is legendary. Buffett acknowledges his debt to Graham in a preface he wrote to the fourth edition of Graham's classic stock-selection guide, *The Intelligent Investor,* regarded as the bible of value managers. 'I read the first edition of this book early in 1950, when I was nineteen,' Buffett wrote. 'I thought then that it was by far the best book about investing ever written. I still think it is ... To me, Ben Graham was far more than an author or a teacher. More than any other man except my father, he influenced my life.'

Sir John Templeton was the founder of the large and very successful Templeton family of mutual funds and one of the very first portfolio fund managers to recognize the value of global investing. Sir John, a Rhodes Scholar, honed his talents under Benjamin Graham. He has been quoted as saying, 'If you are building a house, developing a golf course, or running a doctor's office, you are not in a contest with anyone. But you can't buy a stock unless there's somebody willing to sell it. And because you can't buy unless somebody sells, it's likely that a year later, or five years later, one of you will wish you hadn't done it.' To which he added: 'Because it is a contest, and is therefore different from almost every other business activity on earth, you must not go with the majority. You can gain opportunities in investing only by doing something that the majority are against doing or something they don't know about.' This parallels his oft-quoted admonition to 'buy when others are despondently selling and then sell when others are actively buying.'

Enter Mr Market

Graham invented the figure of Mr Market, who comes to trade with you every day. You can buy at Mr Market's price, you can sell at Mr Market's price, or you can do nothing and wait. The great thing about Mr Market is that he always comes back the next day, giving you the same choices and opportunities.

Mr Market comes to trade each day at prices that are often irrational. How does this happen? In the short run, prices reflect the simple supply and demand of investors. If buying demand exceeds selling supply, prices rise, and if selling supply exceeds buying demand, prices fall. In Benjamin Graham's terms, the market votes on things and comes up with a price. What does it base its vote on? Everything from earnings surprises to rumours about the CEO and institutional factors such as tax-motivated selling, window dressing, and seasonal factors. As the renowned value investor Seth Klarman has said: 'Most day-to-day market price fluctuations result from supply and demand variations rather than fundamental developments.'[8]

Now, it is also important to understand how Mr Market behaves both in the short run and in the long run. In the short run, the market votes on what a stock is worth and Mr Market often gets the prices wrong. However, in the long run, the market weighs outcomes and Mr Market figures it out and gets the prices right.[9]

Since Mr Market sets prices that often do not reflect true value, a good analyst should be able to find stocks trading well below intrinsic value. This leads to the central feature of value investing, namely, that of the 'margin of safety.'

Margin of Safety

A common interpretation of margin of safety is how far below intrinsic value one is paying for a stock. If you believe a stock is worth $20.00 and you can buy it for $12.00, you have a 40 per cent margin of safety. This margin of safety has two important applications.

First, it is used as a measure of risk. Since estimating stock values is an inexact science, the margin of safety indicates how much you can be off in your estimate and still be relatively safe. So at 40 per cent margin of safety you have a very large margin of error. On the other hand, if you buy a stock at what you believe to be its intrinsic value, you would have no margin of safety and consequently a relatively high risk. The margin of safety theoretically protects the investor from both poor decisions and downturns in the market. Graham astutely recognized that, even if you understood and isolated the unique events associated with a company, you would still be subject to all of the systematic economic, financial, and political factors in the marketplace that affect prices. Margin of safety provides mitigation of these risks. Finally, Benjamin Graham did not consider short-term volatility to be a risk factor – in fact, he believed that there was little risk associated with a well-researched stock purchased at a large margin of safety.

Secondly, margin of safety is a measure of expected return. If you can buy a stock worth $20.00 for $12.00 and you have a five-year horizon, your expected rate of return on the stock is 13.3 per cent per annum.[10] This number can be compared to Treasury Bonds to see whether you are being adequately compensated for the risk of owning the share.

Even those investors and money managers who espouse the principles of value investing diverge over how to apply them in practice. At one extreme are the 'deep value' investors. These are people who apply extremely rigorous tests to the process of stock selection. They are not simply looking for companies that are cheap compared to the broad market; they want companies that they can buy for fifty cents on the dollar. That means a focus not on bankrupts but rather on companies whose stocks are trading well below book value. This can happen if a firm has so-called hidden assets on its balance sheet, such as prime urban real estate being carried at book value. Or it may be because the company operates in a sector or a country that is temporarily out of favour. Or it may be because the company is undervalued and a likely takeover target.[11] At the other end of the scale are 'relative value' managers and investors, who assess the reasonableness of a stock's price by comparing it to similar companies in the same type of business.

Value in the Long Run

There is some empirical support for the notion that value investing works over the long term. In 1981 Yale University economist Robert J. Shiller published a startling paper. In an exhaustive examination of security prices and dividend payments spanning the period 1871 through 1979, he found a strong divergence between the market price of the S&P500 and the Dow Jones Industrial Average and the present value of the two indexes.

He found that the NYSE alternated between bullish – that is, vastly overpriced for a few years – and bearish, that is, significantly underpriced for a while relative to the present value of the stock market's cash-dividend income. Since a security is supposed to equal the discounted present value of future dividends, he concluded that stock prices did not fully reflect existing information and that the search for undervalued stocks might be a fruitful one.

Eugene Fama and Kenneth French analysed stock returns over a twenty-seven-year period. They found that, on average, stocks trading in the lowest price/book (P/B) group yielded returns over twice those of stocks grouped in the high price/book zone.[12] They also found that this was a global phenomenon. They examined portfolios based on highest and lowest 30 per cent of P/E and P/B ratios for the period 1975–96 and found that low P/E and low P/B portfolios all over the world, except in Italy, produced the highest returns.[13]

Similarly, studies indicate that stocks trading at with low P/E multiples have tended to yield higher returns than those trading at high P/E multiples. Typically, the finding is a 3 per cent per annum excess return of value stocks over growth stocks, with the excess return a decreasing function of firm size (that is, the small-cap-value stocks had the largest excess returns). Accordingly, the P/E effect has been closely linked with buying low-priced and small-firm (capitalized) shares. This may be due to the fact that small firms are neglected by analysts and institutions.

Behavioural studies have shown that the value world is one where investors don't like to be! Stocks often become undervalued because they have poor track records. The pattern of creating losses for investors has placed those stocks in the 'fallen angel' category. A long history of losses creates distrust and distaste among investors. In other words, the stock has disappointed them enough times that they no longer trust it and so they shun it.

Conclusion

What has the current crisis shown us? It seems to me that two main lessons can be drawn.

Diversification May Not Protect You in the Short Run

The idea of diversifying a portfolio by not putting all of your eggs in one basket goes back to the very roots of investing. Harry Markowitz taught us how to do it – his Nobel Prize-winning work, first published in 1952, showed investors how to build efficient portfolios. Extensions of his work by his doctoral student William Sharpe, and by John Lintner and others, dealt with the positive aspects of building portfolios and how the unique risk associated with an individual company is minimized in a diversified portfolio of securities, leaving instead the systematic pull of the market and the economy as the source of risk and return.

Portfolio theory and its derivative models were normative models – they told us how we as investors are supposed to behave with respect to portfolio diversification. The basic notion is that inclusion of less than perfectly correlated assets reduces risk. However, correlations among equity markets may change in the short run. Markets tend to move together during economic or political shocks (such as the 1987 global market crash or the terrorist attacks of 11 September 2001).[14] It seems that, when the volatility of global markets rises, the correlation between markets increases. Accordingly, very short-term diversification effects may be limited. Markets go their own way – they may react in the very short run to catastrophic events – but ultimately it is the economic outlook, interest rates, and corporate profits that fuel markets, not crises.

Remember the 'Milan Panic' in April 2002 when, on a Thursday trading day around noon EDT, the wire services reported an explosion at the top of a Milan skyscraper in the heart of the financial district. Shortly afterward, Reuters News Service reported that the event was very probably a 'Terrorist Attack.' Global markets plunged on the news. Some fifteen minutes later, the wire services indicated that the crash was most likely an accident and markets rallied, generally recovering all of the losses. What the Milan incident underscores is how interrelated markets are at times of crisis.

In the midst of the financial wreckage in mid-October 2008 was the tale of the tape: the Morgan Stanley Capital International Developed Markets Index[15] of twenty-three countries had lost 38.7 per cent in the year to date and 41.3 per cent over the previous twelve months. What was remarkable was how highly correlated the losses were. Every one of the twenty-three countries had suffered losses – ranging from a low of 28.5 per cent (Japan) to 66 per cent (Ireland). The median loss was 42 per cent. Country diversification had provided virtually no benefit over this period. The sector story was not much better – virtually every sector from consumer discretionary to media was down by 40 per cent to 50 per cent, and very tightly clustered. All of the diversification benefits disappeared during this Black Swan market meltdown as correlations moved closely to 1.

With no benefits from country and sector diversification, could investors look to style for protection? As it turned out – not at all. The value versions of all of the indexes were generally a per cent or so worse than the indexes, the growth versions 1 per cent or so better. To make matters worse, active value managers underperformed the indexes over this period, with some of the legends in the value field racking up their worst short-term records ever.

Of course, asset-class diversification was valuable. Obviously, allocation to fixed income mitigated the losses. But, for long-only equity investors, there was no place to hide.

Value Opportunities Turned Out to Be One Value Trap after Another

The main drawback to value investing from some people's perspective is the emphasis it places on buying out-of-favour stocks that are trading at below the company's break-up value and then waiting un-til the market recognizes the hidden gem and bids the price up to re-alistic levels. Sometimes that process can take a long time, even years, so a portfolio that's built on a value-investing approach may not be at all defensive in the short run. Value managers constantly stress the importance of discipline and patience.

Value investors love to buy great companies selling at bargain prices. In the spring of 2007, many of the financials had moved strongly into bargain territory. The value managers starting buying up the Freddie Macs, the Fannie Maes, Citigroup, Merrill Lynch, Bear Stearns. And as their prices fell they bought more – a bargain is a bigger bargain at a lower price. Perceived margins of safety were 40 per cent, 50 per cent, and more. A case in point. In the winter of 2008 Fannie Mae and Freddie Mac, which own or guarantee almost half of all home loans in the United States,[16] were both well posi-tioned to benefit from the current turmoil in the mortgage market. As one famous value investor described it at the time:

> They are gaining market share, raising credit guarantee fees, imposing stricter underwriting standards and generating higher rates of return on their new investments because of the wider spreads between mortgage rates and their borrowing costs.
>
> However, the market has focused on the write-downs both companies have had to take on their balance sheets. For example, Fannie and Freddie package the vast majority of their mortgages into securities, and accounting regulations require these securities to be 'marked-to-market' – that is as-signed a value based on current market prices. Since the prices of many mortgage-related securities have declined, the companies have suffered some losses on their securities. These are paper losses, though, and they have not changed the fundamental strength of the companies' business

models nor our expectations of their normalized earnings power. Consequently, we believe that Fannie and Freddie are trading at a 70% discount
to fair value – the most undervalued stocks in our universe.

We all know what happened to the two FMs.

During the financial crisis, margins of safety melted away and
value-based portfolios took large hits as the financial stocks in particular led the market meltdown. Time will tell whether this has
created the bargains of a lifetime, as some value investors believe.

NOTES

1 The Dow is a narrow and poorly constructed index of thirty large and very large U.S.
   companies. However, it is the most widely followed index in the world and usually
   proves to be a window on global market events and pricing.
2 All based on closing levels.
3 EAFE is the Europe Australasia and Far East Index and includes twenty-one major developed country markets, not including Canada and the United States.
4 The Dow lost 11 per cent in September 2002, its worst single-month loss in sixty-five
   years.
5 Negative amortization means that the borrower's loan principal is increasing.
6 In many U.S. states mortgage loans are non-recourse, which means that the borrower's
   other assets, if any, are immune from seizure.
7 In contrast, home-price appreciation means that the homeowner's equity is rising and
   increases the likelihood that he/she will continue to make his/her mortgage payments.
8 Seth A. Klarman, *Margin of Safety* (New York: HarperBusiness 1991), 12.
9 In other words, the market is short-term inefficient but long-term efficient. This idea
   of long-term efficiency is important since it means that the stock will eventually move
   to what it is really worth.
10 Ignoring compounding.
11 One of Canada's best-known deep-value managers, Peter Cundill, produced hand-
   some profits for investors in his Mackenzie Cundill Value Fund in 2000–1 when he
   loaded up with shares in high-quality Japanese companies at bargain-basement prices.
12 Eugene Fama and Kenneth French, 'Cross-section of Expected Returns,' *Journal of Finance*, 47, no. 2 (1992): 427–65.

13 Eugene Fama and Kenneth French, 'Value versus Growth: The International Evidence,' *Journal of Finance,* 53, no. 6 (1998): 1975–99.

14 For example, on 10 September 2001 the Dow Jones Industrial Average closed at 9,605. The terrorist attacks occurred the next morning before the market opened. The New York Stock Exchange didn't resume trading until a week later, on Monday, 17 September, when it opened at 9,294 and then fell sharply, ultimately closing at 8,920, down 7.1 per cent from the pre-attack close. The twenty-three-country Morgan Stanley Capital International Developed Markets Index lost just over 8 per cent in that period and markets in general recorded losses in the order of 5 per cent to 10 per cent in the wake of 9/11.

15 Total return index including dividends.

16 The two government-sponsored enterprises were taken over by the U.S. government in September.

5

FINANCIAL ANALYSIS

Integrative Thinking (or Lack of) and the Current Crisis

Ramy Elitzur

In February 2008 one of the guest speakers in Value Investment, the course taught by my colleague, Eric Kirzner, claimed that the subprime crisis was over and thus he could now shift his entire portfolio to Citigroup. Several of my students in Financial Statement Analysis, the second-year elective that I teach in the Rotman MBA program, have approached me and asked for my opinion. My response was that the subprime crisis, far from being over, is in a relatively early stage.

It should be noted that, while the crisis was predictable, I failed to predict either its timing or its extent. Having made that mea culpa, I will provide in this chapter the reasons behind my assessment that the crisis is still with us, and will be for some time to come. I will also present my view of the underlying causes of the crisis, namely, opportunistic and bounded-rationality decision making, or lack of integrative thinking, by several actors in this game. (Avoiding the pitfall of bounded rationality and, instead, making rational, well-reasoned decisions is one of the dimensions of integrative thinking at Rotman.) In addition, this chapter will make some observations on the how this crisis will likely develop in the months ahead, as well as offering a few policy recommendations.

Some Basic Concepts

In order to understand the underlying causes of the current crisis, we need to examine the dynamics of the game played in this context by the various players. These players exhibited two problems that we often discuss in accounting, economics, and finance: the agency problem and bounded rationality (or, as my colleague John Oesch sometimes refers to it, temporal myopia). The agency problem, simply put, is self-interested or opportunistic behaviour by an agent in his or her relationship with a principal. This problem, for example, explains some of the recent accounting scandals, where executives chose to manipulate financial reports in order to maximize their own payoffs (ultimately at the expense of shareholders, unfortunately). The term 'bounded rationality' was first coined by the Nobel Laureate Herbert Simon and later elaborated upon by Amos Tversky and Daniel Kahneman (who also won a Nobel Prize for his work). It describes the tendency of people to make decisions that maximize short-term payoffs at the expense of their long-term welfare. In short, people just want to 'get by' rather than use a rational long-term optimization framework. A related term is 'Satisfice,' that is, the combination of satisfy and suffice, or myopic decision making in the temporal sense. Going back to the earlier example of the accounting scandals, it seems that the managers' decisions involved bounded rationality in that they preferred short-term increases to their compensation over a longer-term perspective.

How the Game Was Played (or Lack of Integrative Thinking Can Be Hazardous to Your Health)

Before I describe the game, I would like to point out that this is a highly stylized and oversimplified version of reality; the oversimplification and stylizing is done to obtain some insights on what precipitated the events we are now experiencing. As such, this is more an informal description than a formal model of the game that took place. Another important feature of the game sketched here is that it has to be examined in a multi-period setting (otherwise, bounded rationality is irrelevant).

The dynamics of this game unfold as follows.

The First Period: First Generation Subprime Loans

In the first period, a high-risk (subprime) borrower approaches a mortgage broker to borrow money for a house. The mortgage broker has a vested interest in getting the mortgage because it involves getting a fee. The borrower has a vested interest in getting the loan so he or she can buy the house. Both of these players are willing to forgo the long-term implications of their decisions since they just want to 'get by.' Both the mortgage broker and the borrower also use faulty reasoning in their thinking, believing that, because real estate prices have been on the rise in the past, they will continue to rise in the future. The mortgage broker and borrower, therefore, agree on a variable rate mortgage where the payments for the first two years are significantly lower than afterwards. The borrower is willing to take this risk because, as he or she mistakenly reasons, in two years prices will go up and, if worse comes to worst, the house can be sold for a gain.

The mortgage broker applies to a financial institution for the loan, shading it strongly by his or her own bias to get it. The person at the lending institution has a vested interest in seeing this through (to get this year's bonus) and has no long-term rational perspective whatsoever. The financial institution's employee also mistakenly reasons that the risk is well managed because the loan is backed by an asset ('What can go wrong? This house can only appreciate').

Next, this mortgage needs to be financed. So the financial institution approaches investors and sells the mortgage to them as part of a package that includes not just this subprime loan but other higher-quality securities. The investors make their decisions on the premise again that mortgages carry high return and subprime mortgages carry much higher yield owing to the inherent risk. Thus, the investors are semi-happy but still not convinced. In order to convince them, the financial institution either buys from another party, or creates on its own, an insurance for this security. In order to avoid the regulation involved with the term 'insurance,' a new term is created, a 'credit default swap,' which offers insurance against default of the security but has no regulation attached to it whatsoever. In particular, the insurer does not need to satisfy the same funding requirements that are mandated by insurance regulators. Why would the insurer take part in such an adventure? Again, short-term gain is the key, as well as the idea that the security is backed by a valuable asset. Now the investor is a 'happy camper' – the money is provided and the loan is made. Throughout the first year, payments are made by the borrower (at a reduced rate) and so all players are happy.

The accounting rule for such securities requires that they should be valued at their fair market value (the rule is also known as 'marked to market'). In the absence of a market for such securities, the rule becomes 'marked to model' and unrealized gains are shown with respect to this security.

The Second Period: Second-Generation Subprime Loans

Here the game is played similarly to the first period but with one major difference: the mortgage broker is now willing to take on an even worse credit risk since he or she, having succeeded in the first period, has grown even more emboldened. The financial institution's employee, the investor, and the insurer (through the credit default swap) all go along because again they all stand to gain: the loan is secured by an asset, and house prices continue to appreciate. Any potential concern is alleviated by the existence of the credit default swap and by the fact that the borrower in the first period is making payments. And so in the second period the quality of the synthetic security is worse than in the first one. The fair-value accounting treatment at this point once more shows gains.

The Third Period: A Perfect Storm

In this period the first-generation borrower is facing difficulties meeting the escalated mortgage payments, which are well above what he or she can afford based on his or her income. It should also be observed that, at this point, the principal on the loan is higher than when we started because the payments by the borrower covered only part of the interest and no principal. At the same time, real estate prices plunge and thus we face a double whammy – the loan's principal is higher and the value of the house is lower than when we started. The borrower tries to make payments but eventually gives up and, since this is a non-recourse loan (which is standard in most U.S. states), is willing to abandon the house. A non-recourse mortgage means that, as opposed to the situation in Canada, the lender has no claim on the borrower's assets other than the house and therefore cannot force bankruptcy. The lender has no choice but to foreclose on the house, which is worth substantially less than the principal on the mortgage. The lender approaches the provider of the credit default swap to compensate him or her for the loss, but the provider, alas, has not deposited enough money in a fund to cover such losses. The lender still gets money from the insurer but it is clear that we are in the beginning of a subprime crisis. What exacerbates the problem is the fair-market-value accounting rule, which now shows losses (and that 'the emperor is naked'). The accounting losses affect adversely the stock prices of all the securities involved.

Fourth Period: A Meltdown

Here the second-generation loans come back to haunt us. Real estate prices are significantly down, borrowers abandon houses en masse, and the seller of the credit default swap does not have enough money to cover all these losses. At this stage, the accounting losses mount even higher, which, in turn, creates a meltdown in the stock prices for all institutions involved. The financial institutions face a liquidity crisis and the U.S. government (and others) step in. Another interesting development is the suspension of the fair-market-value accounting rule by standard setters in Canada and the United States.

Outlook

When looking at this crisis we need to separate the U.S. and the Canadian markets because, while the U.S. situation has a substantial impact on Canada, the financial institutions in both countries differ in some significant respects. First, the Canadian banking system is more concentrated than the U.S. one. Consequently, while banking in Canada is more expensive than in the United States, the system is much more stable and more resilient than its American counterpart. Secondly, the exposure of the financial institutions to subprime loans in Canada is minimal, and, while Canadian banks have been exposed to such loans in the United States, their exposure level differs and none has been involved in catastrophic risk. Thirdly, because mortgage loans in Canada do not have the non-recourse feature, borrowers will be less inclined to walk away from their homes when things get tough than their U.S. equivalents.

These differences between the United States and Canada notwithstanding, the U.S.-generated crisis has had some negative impact on Canada, for financial institutions here (like their U.S. counterparts) have started tightening credit. This will be felt hardest by small businesses, which will face severe difficulties managing their working capital as a result of the credit crunch. The result may be increased numbers of insolvencies, which, in turn, will adversely affect the economy through jobs lost.

In the United States, there are other issues too. While Congress has approved a bailout package, in reality relatively little of the money has made its way into the system. Consequently, a political decision has been made but is not yet implemented. This problem is obvious to the markets, leading to erratic market behaviour. Additionally, the bailout package will probably be implemented through massive printing of money by the Federal Reserve, leading to inflation. Such inflation, in conjunction with the other well-known woes of the U.S. economy (e.g., government deficits), could cause again the erosion of the U.S. dollar that we have recently seen, a development that will have a negative impact on Canadian exports to the United States.

Does all this mark the end of capitalism, as some people claim? Probably not. First, the alternative is unclear. Secondly, the question itself stems in large part from a misunderstanding of the nature of capitalism. Capitalism is not synonymous with laissez-faire but rather involves, to a certain degree, some government intervention when there are market failures, as is the case with the current crisis.

Lessons to Be Learned and Policy Implications

There is no question that several institutions should reflect on their decision-making framework. Of no one is this more true than the regulators, who completely failed to regulate the credit-default-swap market (the size of this market is unknown because it is unregulated but it is estimated to be well above US$60 trillion).

Other institutions that failed in their decisions in this crisis were the rating agencies, which need to examine how they conducted their business while remaining completely blind to the problem growing up around them. The accounting profession should also look at the way that 'marked to market' works. The problem here, though, is that it is unclear what a better alternative would be, since historical cost might yield even less information.

Lending and screening practices at financial institutions certainly need to be re-examined. This has to involve some changes in compensation practices so as to alleviate the agency and bounded-rationality problems that were discussed above.

With confidence in the financial institutions considerably eroded, one of the objectives of the federal government, both in Canada and in the United states, should be to prevent runs on banks. This can be achieved by instituting, at least temporarily, full insurance of any amounts deposited in the financial institutions both by businesses and individuals. In Canada this gesture will have probably no cash-flow implications for the government because, as was mentioned earlier, our financial institutions are quite healthy. At the same time, while such a move will likely not have adverse effects on government spending, it should reduce uncertainty and provide a tremendous boost to public confidence in the system.

Finally, government should pay attention to the credit crunch faced by many businesses, both in Canada and in the United States. Since reducing the interest rate is a blunt instrument, I would rather like to see greater efforts by the central banks in both countries to ensure that money is flowing to businesses of all sizes.

Conclusion

One of the interesting features of bounded rationality, as it relates to the stock market, is that when things are good the overall market sentiment is that things will never go bad, and when the market is in a free fall no one believes that things will ever turn around. This probably has to do with the fact that we tend to view the future as an extrapolation of the past, and not consider points of discontinuity. Any economic process has its ups and downs, whether it is real estate or the stock market. As a result, while fortunes were lost in this crisis, there is no doubt in my mind that fortunes will also be made both in the stock market and in real estate. In order to achieve this, we should try to avoid the pitfalls of bounded rationality, take a balanced look at the current situation, and understand that the crisis will end at some point and search for some undervalued stocks because markets usually overreact to bad news. In other words, we should use integrative thinking for financial analysis and investments.

6

BUSINESS ECONOMICS

The Financial Crisis of 2008 and
the 'Real' Economy:
Damage but Not Disaster

Peter Dungan

M y task in this discussion of the great financial crisis of 2008 is to consider the impact of the crisis on what I will call the 'real' economy – that is, the economy of GDP growth, employment, inflation (and, perhaps, exchange rates), and related elements. I mean nothing disparaging by referring to the 'real economy' in contrast to the world of finance: it is simply a convenient label. The real and financial economies are intimately linked and it is the nature of that linkage that I propose to discuss.

I should state at the outset that I am by background a macroeconomist who deals with both forecasts and policy issues of this real economy, and distinctly not an expert in finance. I should also state that the breadth of the subject and the brevity of the space allowed do not permit much in the way of nuance. I will be making some rather broad statements and conjectures that would certainly need to be qualified and referenced in a longer format.

The basic thrust of my contribution is that, while the real economy is in for several unpleasant quarters in both Canada and the United States, the impact of the financial crisis will, in my opinion, in no way be the apocalyptic catastrophe that some commentators have portrayed. Indeed, it should be appreciably milder for Canada than our last two serious recessions (1990–2 and 1981–2) and also milder for the United States than its last two serious recessions (1981–2 and 1974–5). (For the United States, it will probably be somewhat worse than the extremely mild recession of 2001.) In particular, while there may be some features of the *financial* situation that resemble the Great Depression, it is frankly silly to suggest that the impact on the real economy will be anything close to that.

I will make five basic points about the interaction of the real and financial economies and about the likely impact of the financial crisis on the real economy over the next year or two.

1) The 'Cycles' of the Real and Financial Economies Are Often Very Different

Though both the real and the financial economies are subject to cycles,[1] the evidence of the last fifty years indicates that cycles in the real economy have been reduced both in amplitude and in frequency, while this is not the case for cycles in the financial economy. Indeed, in the United States the downsizing of cycles in the real economy is referred to as the 'Great Moderation.' When equity and debt crises have arisen in the more recent past, there have been instances when the real economy showed barely any impact at all – most notably in the cases of the equity market crash of 1987 and the Asian crisis of the late 1990s. The financial turbulence caused by the Enron and related scandals in the United States might have contributed to weakness in GDP growth in 2003, but the Iraq War – very much a 'real' phenomenon – clearly also played a key part.

Why are cycles in the real economy at least partially de-coupled from the size and frequency of cycles in the financial world? There is no one answer to this, but contributing factors include

- an overall shift in output and employment to more stable service sectors and away from more volatile manufacturing and primary production;
- increases in the size of government and the 'automatic stabilizers' that go with a large tax system, and features of the 'safety net' such as unemployment insurance; and

- a surer hand on the levers of monetary policy to regulate and smooth the functioning of the real economy.

In sum, despite the severity of the current *financial* crisis, there is no reason to believe, on the basis of history going back well over fifty years, that a *real* crisis of similar magnitude is likely to erupt.

2) Most of the Current Problems of the Real Economy Are 'Real' and Not the Result of the Financial Crisis

All of the above said, it is still the case that the real economy is showing signs of weakness: both the U.S. and Canadian economies have had at least one quarter of negative GDP growth and the U.S. economy in particular has recently shown some important job losses as well. Yet it is important to understand that the slowdown in the real Canadian and U.S. economies, at least thus far, is not primarily the result of the liquidity crisis but is rather based in quite straightforward 'real' problems. In the United States, the primary cause of weak GDP growth and job losses over the last several years is the fact that too many houses were built relative to the sustainable demographic situation. Of course, a major reason for this overbuild was the deficiencies in the mortgage and financial markets that induced excessive demand for housing in the first place. How this came to be is described in Eric Kirzner's contribution to this volume. Once it became clear that the housing stock was too large relative to the number of households that could sustainably afford it, housing construction retreated as did employment in housing construction and related fields and this has brought down overall U.S. GDP growth and employment.

In Canada, real economic weakness has a distinctly different source in that it is primarily due to the run-up over the last several years in the Canadian dollar, which has made our exports less competitive in world markets and has opened the Canadian market to significantly higher import competition. More recently, of course, weakness in the U.S. market has also spilled over into Canadian foreign trade. In the immediate future it may also be the case that Canada is facing an overall excess of inventories that will need to be sold off before production is increased, thereby further curtailing GDP growth for several quarters.

Finally, it is also likely the case that over the last several years too many automobiles have been purchased in the Canada and the United States relative to a long-term desirable stock. Even had there not been the run-up in oil and gasoline prices that occurred from late 2007 through the middle of 2008 and beyond, it is quite likely that the auto sector would have seen a significant downturn, or at least a pause.

The basic point again from all of this is that the weaknesses in the real U.S. and Canadian economies, at least through September 2008, were largely unrelated to the financial crisis that was in the process of erupting at that time.

3) The Impact of the Liquidity and Equity Crises Is Yet to Come – and It Will Likely Not Be Hugely Negative

If the real economy has shown mostly signs of its own problems through early September 2008, what are likely to be the effects of the liquidity crisis and of the equity market meltdown that have occurred since?

The fall in equity markets is easier to address since we have had a number of examples of this sort of decline before. It is worthwhile remembering that, using the S&P500 Index, the fall-off in equities over the last several months is in roughly the same order of magnitude as the decline that occurred after the 'dot-com' bubble in 2000–1. At that time, as noted above, there was a slowdown but no serious recession in the United States and Canada, and in this earlier episode the much-hyped NASDAQ Index also fell much further than it has currently.

The recent equity slide will certainly have negative effects on business investment (which is more expensive at lower equity prices) and to some extent on consumer spending (with consumers feeling relatively less wealthy as a result of the equity market decline). However, the impact of lower equity prices on consumer behaviour is not likely to be huge if past episodes are any guide. Apparently, many households are either not significantly involved in the equity market or are oblivious to the way in which their pension plans may be involved. History also teaches us that households have often not incorporated recent price increases in their expectations or wealth planning and therefore have less of a downward adjustment to make when equity prices fall.

More worrisome, in the United States context, is the fall in house prices – which is effectively more of a 'real' effect than a financial one. Past studies indicate that consumer wealth and consumption behaviour seem to be more responsive to changes in house prices than to changes in equity prices. Therefore, the significant decline in housing prices in the United States could have a significant short-term impact on U.S. consumers. Nonetheless, it is important to keep in mind that, just as with equity prices, there will likely be a lag effect in many households incorporating both recent price run-ups as well as recent price declines in their expectations and estimates of household wealth. Many U.S. households may not have realized, or paid little attention to, how much their house prices had risen over the last several years, and therefore will not be marking down their estimates of household wealth nearly as significantly as might be imagined now that house prices have fallen. On this item, we will have to wait and see, but it is one of the more significant negative factors hanging over the U.S. economic outlook in the near term.

Where we are on new and uncertain ground is in attempting to estimate the effect of the *liquidity crisis* on the real economy. Where the liquidity crisis is apt to bite in terms of the real economy is that consumers and businesses may find it difficult or impossible to borrow at any interest rate. Obviously, this would restrict demand for housing, automobiles, other big-ticket consumer items, and business investment projects. Moreover (something not often discussed in our textbooks), the lack of credit for day-to-day business activities could cause many businesses to face premature bankruptcy with bad timing of payables and receivables, or to prematurely lay off workers and downsize activities in order to conserve cash and make sure they are not caught short by payables/receivables imbalances.

Yet there has so far been little evidence that 'Main Street' businesses have been finding it very difficult to finance day-to-day business activities. Access to consumer credit has apparently been somewhat restricted in the United States, but not in Canada, though even this constraint appears to be relaxing somewhat. It is difficult to tell in the United States whether the liquidity crisis has been holding back demand for housing given all of the other difficulties the housing sector is facing there.

Finally, at the time of writing (early November 2008), it appears that the liquidity crisis is beginning to recede given the huge sums of cash that have been injected into the system by central banks in the United States (first and foremost) and then around the world. And it is possible that the threat was never as great as first imagined. After all, 'Main Street' businesses were not so seriously infected by toxic mortgage-backed debt as were other financial institutions, and a key component of ongoing profitability for many banks is their dealings with non-bank businesses. Attempts to be too ruthless with these ultimate customers would simply have driven them into the hands of other bank competitors – perhaps permanently.

4) Central Banks Are on the Case, and History Shows Their Intervention to Be Effective

It is also important to recall that central banks in the United States, Canada, and now in most other industrialized nations are working actively not only to correct the financial crisis but also to protect as much as possible the real economy. Past evidence indicates that, when central banks are thus motivated, they can have a significant and powerful corrective effect when combating financial shocks to the real economy.

In this respect it is worth briefly reconsidering the two most serious post-war recessions in Canada and the United States. For Canada, those two recessions occurred in 1981–2 and 1990–2. In both cases the recessions were, to a considerable extent, actually induced by the Bank of Canada in order to reduce the rate of inflation. In short, monetary policy was not used to insulate the real economy in these cases – indeed it was used to push down the real economy in order to dampen wage and price pressures. The two most serious post-war recessions in the United States were in 1981–2 and in 1974–5. For the former, the U.S. Federal Reserve was also deliberately reining in the real economy in order to reduce inflation. The 1974–5 recession had nothing to do directly with the financial system but was instead the result of a serious supply-price shock (following the first OPEC oil price increases) to which the U.S. Federal Reserve did not really know how to respond.

The basic point is that when a financial shock hits the real economy, and especially when it threatens the health of the financial system, central banks respond vigorously and their responses have been effective. The single constraint on central bank responses has been excess inflation, and this is why central banks were slow to respond when the real economies of the United States and Canada began to be hit by their respective problems in 2007 – long before the liquidity crisis began. High oil prices and the fact that each economy was, at least in the estimate of the central banks, at or above its full-employment level caused central banks to be very cautious about lowering interest rates and freeing up credit when the initial signs of real economic weakness began to appear. Now, however, with a precipitous retreat of oil prices and other commodity prices around the world, concern about excess inflation has disappeared completely and central banks are not only ensuring sufficient liquidity to the financial markets but are also lowering their key interest rates in order to bolster aggregate demand.

5) Important Real-Economy Market Adjustments Are Under Way

A further reason why the real economies of Canada and the United

States are more likely to suffer discomfort rather than catastrophe over the next four to six quarters, despite the severity of the liquidity crisis and the equity-market downturn, is that important real-economy market adjustments are taking place, or have already occurred.

Foremost among these is a drastic drop in petroleum prices, together with the decreases in many other commodity prices as well – including some food products such as wheat. While this is not particularly good news for Canadian producers of raw materials, the reduction in these prices – and especially in the price of gasoline – replaces important purchasing power in the pockets of the average consumer in both Canada and the United States. Indeed, it has been estimated that the reduction in the price of gasoline through the end of October 2008 amounts to as much as 1 per cent of U.S. GDP being returned to American consumers. This will obviously have important effects in sustaining consumer demand over the next few quarters, and, as mentioned, it alleviates concerns of inflation on the part of central banks and leaves them free to intervene to support the real economy and the financial economy at the same time.

For Canada, a second important adjustment is that the Canadian dollar has fallen significantly from its previous level of near parity with the U.S. dollar. While U.S. demand for Canadian products will be weakened by low growth rates in the United States, the lower value of the Canadian dollar will offset this to some extent by making Canadian goods more competitive in U.S. markets and by reducing the attraction of imported goods in Canadian markets.

Summary – and Lessons to Be Learned

Briefly, the period from the fourth quarter of 2008 and well into

2009 should be a period of very low or modestly negative GDP growth for the Canadian and U.S. economies, and of gradually rising unemployment. Beginning in the second half of 2009, a gradual recovery should begin as adjustments are made in response to the shocks hitting the economies. GDP growth in 2010 may in fact be quite strong as the output 'gap' between actual and potential production that opened in 2008–9 begins to be closed, and unemployment rates in the two countries should begin to fall again.

If this comes to pass, it will clearly not be a disaster. I contend that the 'real' economy will endure the liquidity crisis and the equity-market crash of 2008 with only this relatively modest damage primarily because the real economy demonstrates remarkable resilience in the face of financial-sector shocks, and because central banks, and their associated governments, have taken timely and massive action to head off a worse crisis. Moreover, part of the grief that the U.S. and Canadian real economies will suffer over the next year is not fundamentally due to the financial 'crisis' at all but rather to imbalances and other adjustments that would have taken a toll in any event – most important, the overbuild of the U.S. housing stock (which, it is true, had its roots in a badly regulated financial system), and the adjustment in Canada to an overall higher level of the Canadian dollar compared to the previous two decades (and despite the short-term reprieve that the recent decline in the Canadian dollar affords the economy).

An important theme of this volume is 'lessons to be learned.' Primarily, these lessons are for the financial sector, and other contributors have made some important diagnoses and have suggested prescriptions for the ills of the financial sector which would do much to head off a repeat of the current crisis. In my opinion, the chief lesson to be learned on the *real* side of the economy is to maintain even greater vigilance for serious imbalances in the stocks of real goods. Twice now, in less than ten years, the U.S. economy in particular has overbuilt its stocks of physical assets. In the late 1990s and into 2000, there was over-investment in information-technology equipment (with the accompanying 'dot-com' financial bubble). When it was realized that too much such equipment had been accumulated, the economy entered a mild recession, while there was a major equity-market correction. Gradually the excess stock was worked off and the economy recovered. From 2005 to 2007, the United States overbuilt its housing stock, with an accompanying housing-price bubble, and with the financial implications we are now well aware of. This bubble, too, has burst, with another accompanying equity crash. The effect on housing stock will take longer to work off (houses last longer than IT equipment), but there are other ways of employing the capital and labour that are used to build houses – perhaps in repairing key infrastructure in the United States that is under increasing stress. Canada, too, will face a milder retrenchment in housing and has also to deal with a shift away from manufacturing.

For what it is worth, a clear lesson is to watch for these sorts of real imbalances and, if possible, take steps to rein them in. This is easier said than done, since often imbalances do not become apparent as such until they are well along and who, after all, wants to argue that there is too much productive investment being made in a new technology, or too much good housing being made available to people who previously could not afford it? Nonetheless, we all must do what we can to call attention to such issues, and to argue for more balance and less haste in the evolution of our real economies in the future.

NOTE

1 Personally, I prefer the less-scientific 'ups and downs' to 'cycles' because the latter connotes too much of a regular or predictable mechanism causing the cyclical movements. In my view, there is relatively little regularity to the 'ups and downs' of either economy; instead, 'stuff happens.' I will use 'cycles' for brevity and because it is more familiar.

7

INTERNATIONAL BUSINESS

Global Lessons from the 2008 Financial Crisis

Wendy Dobson

The current crisis is the latest in a long series of financial crises that stretch back into the mists of time. But it is one of the first truly global crises in which all open economies have felt its effects. Our responses should recognize that, while we cannot eliminate boom and bust, careful regulatory responses can reduce their frequency and magnitude. Modern financial systems provide uniquely useful services. They reduce information asymmetries between borrowers, who know a lot about their ability to repay loans on time and in full, and lenders, who do not. They facilitate payments in economic exchange; mobilize and pool savings; acquire and process information about enterprises and investment projects; help direct savings to productive uses; diversify and reduce risks; and monitor investments in enterprises as well as the performance of their managers. During the past three decades, capital has flowed ever more freely across borders, facilitated by advances in information technology, deregulation, and financial innovation. Borderless capital has left national regulators scrambling to catch up. Regulators not only lost the race in the current crisis but played significant roles in creating the problem. Governments face a new question: Are diverse national regulators consistent with a single global capital market?

Every financial crisis is different. The 1997–8 Asian crisis began as a currency crisis in Thailand where the central bank tried to maintain a fixed exchange rate in spite of a large current-account deficit, rapidly became a financial crisis when the country ran out of foreign-exchange (FX) reserves and had to hike interest rates, and then became an economic crisis as borrowers defaulted, businesses failed, and unemployment soared. Thailand's neighbours were caught up in the contagion as confidence evaporated.

The trigger for the current crisis was a slowdown and then decline in U.S. housing prices but some of its roots can be traced back to the Asian crisis. Asian governments, still smarting from the agonies of the crisis a decade earlier, managed their exchange rates for stability and in the process built up huge FX reserves. Most of these reserves were invested in low-risk U.S. government bonds. U.S. monetary policy was easy for a prolonged period and interest rates low. In this environment, U.S. financial markets came to assume that housing prices would always rise amid a mythical attachment, espoused by interest groups and politicians, to universal home ownership. No one asked what might happen if house prices were to fall.

Lax regulation and financial innovation played key roles in turning this opportunity into a problem. Low interest rates encouraged financial innovation as investors 'reached for yield.' Mortgage lenders were able to use financial innovations such as asset securitization to transfer the risks rather than hold the mortgages and face the attendant risks of default as they had in the past. In this new environment, mortgage lenders had no incentive to monitor creditworthiness and took more risks, supposedly distributing them to others more willing to bear them. No one kept track of the distribution, and risk turned out to have remained more concentrated than anyone realized.

Government-sponsored entities charged with lending and insuring mortgages, Fannie Mae and Freddie Mac, were overseen by a government agency – an arrangement that created significant moral hazard: the perception of a government guarantee which led to low borrowing costs despite the enormous leverage that eventually brought them down. Capital-adequacy requirements set cooperatively by central banks working together at the Bank for International Settlements (BIS) were a factor as well. In the wake of the Asian crisis, banks were required to increase the capital on their balance sheets against a wider range of lending activities. In response, banks used financial innovations to set up complex off-balance-sheet structures aimed at offsetting these requirements. At the same time, in the United States an entire 'shadow' banking system grew up consisting of investment banks, private equity and hedge funds, and money managers which relied on short-term institutional funding rather than retail deposits and so went unregulated. Freed of capital requirements, these institutions engaged in breathtaking amounts of leverage, not only enlarging the risks but intensifying the financial markets' procyclical behaviour. This, in turn, exposed the markets to negative shocks because of the speed with which they had to deliver when things went wrong.

Leverage is still being unwound as banks short of capital call in their loans to hedge funds, as U.S. investment banks disappear through merger and bankruptcy, and as Goldman Sachs and J.P. Morgan turn themselves into holding companies subject to the same regulations as commercial banks. These changes were not mandated by regulators, they were forced by market participants responding to lack of transparency and the uncertainty linked to the complexity of the new instruments.

When disaster struck, the scale of risks and their concentration were surprising to many. Regulators knew much of what was going on but failed to estimate the potential magnitude of the consequences. Uncertainty prevailed and with it lack of trust. In the absence of transparency, liquidity dried up and institutions and markets stopped functioning.

What are the lessons? Going forward, will we be able to enjoy the advantages of open capital markets while also enjoying reasonable economic stability? I believe we can but immediate and longer-term lessons must be drawn.

One immediate lesson is that we do know how to stop a banking crisis. After a false start in the United States, the sure-footed British approach addressed both liquidity and solvency problems by dealing with troubled assets, thawing out frozen inter-bank markets with guarantees, and addressing capital adequacy by injecting liquidity into banks in exchange for bank equity. This approach was also designed to minimize moral hazard; participation in the rescue was voluntary and costly conditions were imposed on those institutions that did.

Another immediate lesson is that the procyclical elements of the system must be rethought. Not least, lower levels of leverage seem to be called for, off-balance-sheet activities need to be disciplined, and the costs and benefits of mark-to-market accounting should be reconsidered.

A third lesson relates to the role of central banks in preventing crises. Current orthodoxy is that price stability should be the single goal of central banks, one that they achieve with their single instrument, monetary policy. Yet they are the lender of last resort in a crisis. The quid pro quo – bank regulation – is often performed by another entity. The question raised by this crisis is whether central banks, which are responsible for financial stability, need a stake in the second instrument, bank regulation, to perform their function as lenders of last resort. That way, in a crisis, they would hold the cards they require, but, more significantly, they would have the intimate knowledge of local banks that they need to head off problems at early stages. Resistance can be expected to such a proposal, not least in the United Kingdom, which led the way towards a single regulator separated from the Bank of England. The regulator coordinates with the Bank of England but the Northern Rock failure shows the limits to coordination. While Canada's structure is similar, the recent outcome was more reassuring because its banks were less exposed.

The longer-term agenda is a large one. Should global capital and financial markets have a single global financial supervisor, or at least a single regulatory framework? Transparent information and accurate prices are the lifeblood of efficient markets. This was apparent after the Asian financial crisis when a start was made with the Financial Stability Forum, supported by the BIS, whose mandate is to promote closer cooperation among national bodies responsible for supervising financial institutions such as insurance, securities, and foreign-exchange markets. Bodies responsible for financial infrastructure such as credit-rating agencies and accounting standards were also involved. In the wake of the current crisis, we will see more effort to create universal standards. We can expect closer scrutiny of, even standards of practice for, the purveyors of market information such as the rating agencies. We can also expect to see tighter scrutiny of bank management and boards of directors. And we can expect to see attention to other issues that have violated popular perceptions of fairness, such as short selling and excessive executive compensation.

Political leaders' rhetoric, particularly in Europe, notwithstanding, we are unlikely to see a global super-regulator for at least two reasons. First, governments are not about to give up national sovereignty to create one. Consider how national-sovereignty considerations hampered the efforts of European Union member governments to coordinate a coherent area-wide response. Their first meeting ended in disagreement and discord and the second one was driven by pressures from G-7 governments and from the urgency injected by Prime Minister Gordon Brown. The immediate need, rather, is for a coherent framework that achieves the same ends in diverse national economies. This is not an impossible task. It has already been achieved by central banks whose governors meet regularly in unremarked meetings at the BIS and who, as long ago as the 1987 financial crisis, demonstrated their ability to work together quickly and seamlessly to support global liquidity. Their record is not perfect, however; they do not seem to have been able to convince U.S. monetary authorities to tighten lax monetary policy in recent years, nor have they been able to convince the Chinese government that its central bank's heavy focus on exchange-rate management creates global as well as domestic distortions and imbalances.

The second reason relates to the arguments favouring the provision of central banks with more cards to play in preventing banking crises. To be effective, regulators need to be very knowledgeable about the institutions they oversee. A global regulator cannot meet this criterion. Size and reach cannot make up for the necessary proximity and focus. In North America, for example, we have seen the unintended consequences of such consolidation in a much different institution, the Department of Homeland Security. Tasked with a unified approach to securing the homeland, it is busy building barriers to trade.

We are, however, witnessing the return of government. This should not be a surprise. But it is worrisome. Open capital markets create opportunities but also pose large risks. Since the Reagan and Thatcher revolutions in the 1980s, the state has accepted the discipline of the market and has moved back to being the rule setter and the referee. We are now seeing predictable reconsideration in response to widely held perceptions that sophisticated financial markets deliver instability instead of growth and, at least in executive compensation, unfairness.

Bank regulation will be tightened. Government ownership was essential in the financial rescues but is cause for worry. Such ownership is likely to be temporary in the United Kingdom. In the United States, the ad hoc approach in which even strong banks were compelled to participate is now picking winners and losers. How much bureaucratic intervention in bank strategy and daily decision making will there be before government sells its stakes? In major emerging market economies where government ownership is a fact of life, delays in privatization will contribute to high costs of capital for small entrepreneurial enterprises. The Indian government's long-standing commitment to reduce its ownership stakes in 2009 has been put on hold. The Chinese government still owns all large banks, which lend mainly to yesterday's industries – a pattern that is now less likely to change.

Is there need for more government intervention? Do the costs in terms of instability of liberalized and open financial markets outweigh the benefits of faster growth and improvement in economic efficiency? In the past twenty years, available evidence from cross-country studies shows that countries with deeper and more sophisticated financial systems have grown faster because capital can be allocated more efficiently. Individual welfare is promoted when households can obtain credit to smooth their consumption requirements through time. Against this evidence must be weighed such effects as the impact of the bursting U.S. housing bubble on those least able to bear such costs and the impact on confidence and growth of procyclical lending patterns exacerbated by the leveraging practices of the shadow banking system.

The costs, however, should be associated with deficiencies of national regulatory systems, particularly in the United States, not with liberalized and open financial markets. There was no consolidated supervision of investment banks or insurers and no effective regulation of mortgage brokers, to mention a couple of the most obvious weaknesses. Regulators remained wedded to frameworks that provided unintended incentives for off-balance-sheet entities, with mark-to-market accounting that was procyclical. To be fair, they warned of some of the consequences but no one listened.

Grand ideas about restructuring the global financial architecture will be discussed among the world's leaders. These statements should be heard more as code words for closer cooperation among governments and better regulatory institutions in the United States and Europe. The central challenge is better regulation and fewer loopholes created by differing regulatory regimes – not the building of international architecture. The level of ambition is laudable but rhetoric will be tempered by the reality that most of what is needed already exists – it needs to be made more effective and legitimate in preventing crises and managing them if they do occur.

As well, two institutions, the G-7 and the International Monetary Fund (IMF), should be restructured to become more relevant. The G-7 could acquire legitimacy as an 'international executive committee' if its membership were broader. At least China, India, Brazil, and South Africa should be added to its ranks. The IMF has the necessary expertise and near-universal membership to be the lender of last resort. But it no longer has the resources and clout in part because private capital flows now hugely exceed public flows. It has also fallen on hard times because of perceptions that it mishandled the Asian financial crisis and because its governing structure still largely reflects countries' economic importance sixty years ago rather than today. Yet the IMF has had experience with 122 banking crises. It has a number of emergency finance mechanisms. Its tools for conducting macroeconomic surveillance can be used to track cross-country financial and economic linkages. Its Financial Sector Assessment Programs are credible and comprehensive and should be linked into international forums and national regulators. The IMF's warnings of impending problems in its surveillance reports and semi-annual surveys of the world economy went largely unheeded. Iceland's predicament and those of other emerging market economies suffering from secondary effects have underlined the IMF's central importance as the international lender of last resort.

Finally, the focus to date on the financial system is necessary but not sufficient. The impacts on growth in the broader economy will be serious, through rising unemployment, deflation, currency volatility, and possibly protectionism. The degree of uncertainty in financial markets will take time to overcome. U.S. house prices will eventually stop falling and consumers will repair their balance sheets. Until then, the negative fallout in the U.S. economy will be substantial, with exports the only bright spot. Growth is slowing in other regions and major economies and they are unlikely to replace the U.S. consumer as the engine of global growth in the next few quarters. How long will the U.S. dollar resist further depreciation? This is due to the repatriation of capital to the United States to repair balance sheets as well as a flight to quality. But the trend is not likely to continue. The size of the future U.S. fiscal deficit is unknown except that it is 'stratospheric,' both because of the size of spending commitments ('whatever it takes') and because revenues are shrinking. The deficit is unlikely to continue to be financed by foreign central banks' purchase of U.S. bonds so the financing will have to come from higher savings by U.S. households and corporations, or from inflation. Another worrisome side effect is the growing perception that globalization is bad for the American middle class. Democrats preparing to take both houses of Congress and the presidency are pandering to protectionist sentiment. It will be difficult, however, to avoid the messages now coming out of congressional hearings that American regulators, rather than foreigners, contributed to the financial crisis.

Despite these very real concerns, it is useful to recall that crises also create opportunities. The lessons from the 1930s demonstrate the disastrous consequences of trade protectionism and lack of mutual trust and cooperation among governments. Nationalism and protectionism trumped the global public interest and the crisis deepened. The opportunity ahead is clear. Governments have shown signs that they recognize the advantages of closer economic coordination in which, by carrying out sound policy adjustments at home, they contribute to a common global solution. The G-7 action plan endorsed on 10 October 2008 laid out sound basic principles which, when the seven governments then coordinated their rescue activities, restored some semblance of confidence to markets.

But we should have no illusions. Financial institutions will continue to innovate and financial regulators will continue to be one step behind. There is a very real danger that governments, acting in haste for political reasons, will do long-term damage through excessive or ill-advised intervention. When regulators and the IMF warn of impending problems during the next boom, politicians and market participants should listen and regulators should act. But will they?

8

CORPORATE GOVERNANCE

Where Were the Directors?

David R. Beatty

We are in the midst of a tectonic-plate movement in the financial world that now appears to be shaking the 'real' world quite dramatically. The purpose of this chapter is not to review the causes and potential consequences of our current situation but to explore the possibility that once again, in the world of publicly traded companies, boards of directors have let us down.

A Long Look Back

If we go back to the bursting of the South Sea bubble in London in 1720, we can record the first time shareholders bellowed this refrain: 'Where were the directors?' Following the collapse of the Great South Seas Corporation (and many other companies also publicly traded at that time), Alexander Pope wrote a sonnet that began 'At length corruption, like a general flood, / Did deluge all, and avarice creeping on, / Spread, like a low born mist and hid the sun' and ended with the sad conclusion that 'Britain was sunk in lucre's sordid charms.' The British Parliament acted swiftly, putting many directors in jail, taking over their estates, and banning joint-stock companies for one hundred years.

In *The Way We Live Now*, nineteenth-century novelist Anthony Trollope wrote about the board of the magnificently named Great South Central Pacific and Western Railway Company as follows: 'The Chairman, Augustus John Melmotte himself, would speak a few slow words ... always indicative of triumph, and then everybody would agree to everything, somebody would sign something, and the board would be over.' John Galsworthy in the Forsyth saga records Soame Forsyth asking in *The White Monkey*, 'What, besides the drawing of fees and the drinking of tea, were the duties of a director?' And finally, Irving Olds, the chair and CEO of U.S. Steel in 1940, declared that directors were 'the parsley on the fish – decorative but not useful.' Perhaps he was right.

Modern Times

Following the market crash of 1929 and the Great Depression that ensued, a revolution in oversight and regulation of public markets occurred under President Franklin D. Roosevelt. The Securities and Exchange Commission was established and stock exchanges dramatically tightened their listing requirements.

Fast forward to 2001 and the failures of Enron, Worldcom, Adelphia, and a clutch of others companies including Conrad Black's Hollinger Ltd, listed in Toronto, and its subsidiary Hollinger Inc., listed in New York, when once again the question surfaced: 'Where were the directors?' These failures resulted in the tectonic plates of regulatory reform moving again for the first time in over seventy years. The Sarbanes-Oxley Act of 2002 (known as SOX) created dramatic changes in the way modern, publicly traded companies must govern themselves.

Figure 8.1, examines the typical structure of an American board prior to Sarbanes-Oxley. In this simple model, the shareholder elects the board; the board selects the CEO, and the CEO picks his/her team. The board then delegates the management of the corporation to the CEO while looking after compensation matters and maintaining a general oversight of the company. At the same time as the directors are elected, the shareholders select an auditor who independently examines the books and reports back to the Audit Committee of the board and then to the shareholders. The report of the

Figure 8.1
Corporate governance: The theory

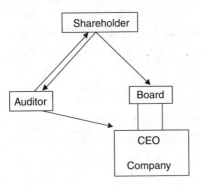

Figure 8.2
Corporate governance: The reality

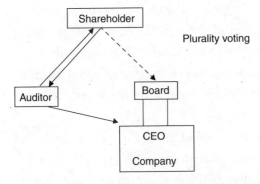

auditors is intended to provide the shareholders an unvarnished account of the true state of the financial affairs of the corporation.

That's the theory, anyway, but prior to the scandals of 2001 things did not actually work this way. As shown in Figure 8.2, there was some blurring of the lines: The first anomaly in this structure is that, in both Canada and the United States, but nowhere else in the world, shareholders are given a choice of voting 'for' the director candidate or 'withholding' their vote from that candidate. This means that you need only one vote 'for' to be elected. This perverse system is called 'plurality voting' and is in stark contrast to the rest of the world, which embraces 'majority voting.' Under majority voting, you vote 'for' or 'against' a director candidate, and to get elected you need more votes 'for' than 'against.'

So, in a very real sense, in Canada and the United States, shareholders do not elect their directors. Instead, they bless the proposals put forward essentially by the board chair. It's a system more reminiscent of a Soviet tradition than a democratic tradition: 'Here's the slate – approve it!'

There is a second anomaly. In 80 per cent of American companies, the CEO is also the chair of the board. In Canada the number is reversed, with 80 per cent of publicly traded companies having a chair of the board independent of the CEO. The rest of the world looks more like Canada than the United States. The practical consequence is that, in the United States, the chair selects his/her board to oversee him/her. 'How can the fox be put in charge of the henhouse?' is a common reaction.

Two consequences flow from these anomalies. First, with the chair selecting the director candidates and the shareholders not being able to vote against the directors, it is often (though not always) the case that an 'Imperial CEO' emerges who essentially is responsible to no one but him/herself. Neither the check nor the balance assumed by the shareholder's election of the board is in place. Second, the ability of the auditor to examine independently the finances of the corporation is seriously compromised. The possibility exists that the CEO, acting as chair, might also select the chair of the Audit Committee. Further, the auditor might, for all practical purposes, be deemed to report to the chief financial officer, who might also ad-

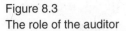

Figure 8.3
The role of the auditor

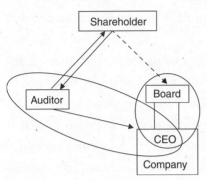

vise the Audit Committee on the terms under which the auditor should be hired (see Figure 8.3).

Prior to Sarbanes-Oxley, there was no clear distinction between 'auditor' and 'corporate executive'; a fog of conflict had descended, obscuring the separation of duties and responsibilities upon which shareholders rely. This obfuscation rendered it awkward, if indeed at all possible, to have an unbiased and independent view of the financial affairs of the corporation.

Then, almost immediately following the disclosures surrounding Enron, WorldCom, and Adelphia, the U.S. Congress acted to reform the consequences of the anomalies mentioned above. At their most basic, the SOX reforms ensured the separation of the auditor from the management of the company and clearly established that the auditor worked for and was paid by the board's Audit Committee and reported independently to shareholders through that committee. To ensure that there was a further check on the auditor/company relationship, the auditors' historic right to regulate their own profession was stripped away, and a Public Company Accounting Oversight Board (PCAOB, known colloquially as 'Peekaboo') was put in place. The PCAOB, among its many duties, must certify any audit company working for publicly traded corporations. Without that certification, the audit company is not eligible to perform work in a publicly traded firm.

A vast array of details was also included in the SOX legislation, including CEO/CFO certification of the accounts, under the threat of criminal prosecution. At its very core, SOX transformed the nature of the auditing profession's relationship to the corporation that it audited. This reform, in the American context, was sorely needed.

SOX also had three major effects on American boards that spilled over to corporate Canada as well. First, the chair of the Audit Committee had to have solid financial credentials and members of the audit committee were expected to be 'financially literate.' No more earnest amateurs allowed. Second, the work of the board in its oversight functions, particularly the review of the financial accounts, became much more detailed. The average American board began to spend significantly more time in the boardroom and in preparation for the boardroom. Estimates vary widely, but some observers suggest that the average time spent as a director of a major American company increased from 250 to 350 hours a year. Third, because of the heavy overlay of regulatory approval, the time spent by directors was shifted towards regulatory and oversight matters and away from longer-term work such as helping management develop strategy and talent.

In a survey done jointly by the Canadian Coalition for Good Governance (CCGG) and McKinsey in 2004, some 275 directors estimated their time allocation from two perspectives: as they found it to be and as they wished it to be. Figure 8.4 shows the results. Today, most boards continue to work approximately 350 hours a year

Figure 8.4
How should directors invest their time?

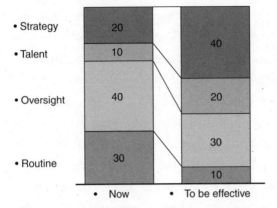

but have effectively absorbed the SOX burdens and are gradually shifting their time back to strategy and talent development.

The Impact of the Financial Crisis

Having only recently recovered from the SOX reforms, boards now not only have to navigate the troubled credit and liquidity waters of the financial tsunami but also face the prospect of yet more governance reforms. This will be especially true in the financial-services sector. I expect that there will be one new reform that boards will need to address and two 'old chestnuts' that will remain a constant challenge: 1) ensuring that the board has the requisite skills, particularly in risk management and in compensation; 2) managing directors' time more effectively; and 3) spanning the information chasm effectively.

Just as SOX imposed skill requirements upon directors serving on Audit Committees, I am confident that a call will be raised for at least one director – especially in financially regulated institutions – to have had direct line experience with risk management. There may also be requirements for the Risk Management Committee to be composed only of 'risk literate' directors, to be independently 'audited,' and to report to shareholders separately from the auditor's report on the risk-management practices of the board.

There is a good chance that boards will have to specifically address their competence to set compensation. The need for independent and unconflicted advice to the Compensation Committee will be further emphasized. As it happens, the compensation-advisory industry is dominated by firms who provide many compensation services to company executives (for example, pension-fund calculations). There will likely be a much more pronounced push to ensure that the board gets advice from non-conflicted advisers and that those advisers work for and report only to the chair of the Compensation Committee. Such arrangements would mimic the relationships of the auditor to the Audit Committee after SOX.

In general, I would expect to see boards move to a more 'expert' model. SOX imposed the financial expert; the current crisis will likely establish the need for a risk expert on the board and possibly a compensation expert. But, to be an effective contributor to strategy, a board must also contain subject-matter experts. The task is certainly not to meddle with management but to increase the likelihood that boards can contribute to management's thinking about future strategic direction.

The day of the all-amateur board that flies over at 50,000 feet and Mach 2 is gone. Directors need to be able to ask more than generic questions: 'What is the competition doing?' 'How will this affect the employees?' 'Have you thought about X and Y?' Insight into strategy in a fast-moving and globally competitive business demands directors who actually know something about the business which they are supposedly overseeing in the interests of the shareholders.

Most boards do not track how their directors invest their time, even by the rudimentary categories shown above. The old managerial saying that 'If you can't measure it you can't manage it' holds for boards as well. If directors are going to spend their time maximizing their potential to contribute to shareholder well-being, they are going to have to wrestle the allocation of that time away from the mundane and towards the strategic end of the spectrum. There is no chance that a director will want to spend more time being a director – they are already 'maxxed out.' Changing the way directors invest their time is never easy, but there are a few trips gleaned from best practices:

1. Ask the corporate secretary to keep a simple running tally of how the board is investing its time. This tally should be considered by the chair as the agenda is designed for each subsequent meeting.
2. Push as hard as you can to get routine matters dealt with in a 'consent agenda' to free up time for strategic business issues.
3. Ensure papers coming to the board are clear, memorable, and compelling in that they:
   • bring directors into the story;
   • describe the issue you are grappling with;
   • propose the answer; and
   • defend the answer with logical reasons.
4. The better the briefing, the more effective the use of the directors' time, both prior to the meeting and during it. Do not let

executives make PowerPoint presentations at the board meeting. The operative assumption must be that the directors have done their homework and have both read and thought about the materials. The job of the executive is to refer the directors to a few relevant pages of the briefing book to refresh their memory and then get straight into the Q&A dialogue.

The one problem that is common to all boards and all management teams at all times is the spanning of the information chasm between managers and directors. A manager spends perhaps 3,000 hours a year at work, usually surrounded by other executives labouring just as long. It is also frequently the case that most, if not all, of the senior management team have spent a lifetime in the company or industry where they now work.

Compare that to a director who might annually invest 300 hours in board meetings and preparation. That director will almost always have many other business matters 'on the go,' so there is not a clear and complete focus on the business at hand. What an intellectual conceit it is, then, for a director to 'wander in off the street' for a board meeting and make a contribution to corporate strategy! Or even to make intelligent and informed comment on a particular decision.

How do managements and boards come to terms with this challenge? Or should boards simply stick to their compliance and oversight roles and leave strategy and major decisions entirely to management? Experience has shown that there are techniques and processes that can help directors make more informed and considered decisions that create value for shareholders. Below, I offer a few hints from leading practitioners on how to span this chasm – all derived from the Rotman School's 'Directors Education Programme,' run for the Insititute of Corporate Directors (www.icd.ca).

Maintain the Dialogue

The chair must take the lead to ensure that the dialogue among directors is initiated and maintained. As the meeting begins, the chair should 'formally' enquire about the preparedness of the directors. Then, as the meeting progresses, the chair should note the quality of the dialogue. And, at the end of the meeting, during the 'in camera' session, the chair should explicitly seek out views of the board members on whether or not they felt they had been brought into the picture and were given an opportunity to contribute to the discussion in an informed way.

It is also vital that the chair report back to the CEO and/or the management team following the 'in-camera' session. The wise chair will first canvas opinion from the CEO (or the entire top management team) regarding the meeting. Were the directors engaged? Did management get any new insights or points of view? Did management feel that the board should have weighed things somewhat differently? What kinds of things worked with the board? Where did the board feel uncomfortable? Only when management's points of view are ascertained should the chair give his/her feedback on the board's perspective.

From this dialogue among the directors and between the chair and management, the chair and the CEO must distil opportunities to improve the spanning of the information chasm. Perhaps the briefing books needed more background; perhaps the risks needed to be more carefully explored; possibly the directors wanted more discussion. These adjustments are vital to a longer-term understanding of what works for a board and what doesn't. Only if the chair makes these adjustments, and does so adeptly, is there any hope that the governance-management chasm will be effectively spanned to create long-term value for the shareholder.

Keep Strategy at the Top of the Agenda

Many boards have ensured that they are allocating their time to the most important issues facing their company. Here are some of their practices:

1. Developing a strategic orientation:
   a. building a one/two day off-site strategy session into the annual board-meeting calendar;
   b. getting the directors into a rigorous orientation program; and
   c. Continuously learning about the business, i.e., analysts reports, field visits, conferences, regular updates from CEO, etc.
2. Starting every board meeting with a CEO update, focusing on the following questions:
   d. 'What's different in the environment since we last met?'
   e. 'How might our strategy be adjusted in response – if at all?'
   f. 'What are the things I am looking out for?'
3. Making it one of the chair's tasks to encourage a discussion that is strategic but enquiring and free ranging.
4. Maintaining an inventory of 'strategic issues' and allocating the #2 agenda item (after the CEO update) to one of these issues when possible/necessary.

*Use the 'In Camera' Meetings to Assess How Effectively You Have
Spanned the Chasm*

In the end, spanning the information chasm is the single biggest
challenge for a board that is determined to add value. Facing this
universal problem requires constant attention from both sides. A
simple technique is to use the 'in camera' meetings at the end of each
board to assess the overall, and possibly decision-by-decision, effectiveness of management's presentations and materials in bringing
the directors into the picture. Three questions that need to be asked
are:

- Did the directors feel sufficiently well briefed to have been able
  to come to an informed decision?
- Were the pre-meeting briefing papers models of clarity and structure?
- Was the discussion during the board meeting insightful and di-
  rected?

Conclusion

Boards have been struggling for centuries to represent their shareholders effectively. Intermittent catastrophes have shone a bright
light on the way in which directors have carried out their responsibilities and have led to the now universal question 'Where were the
directors?'

There is no doubt that today's multiple crises will lead to further
evolution in the corporate-governance practices of boards and that

future crises will again raise the bar. In the meantime, boards must work hard at evaluating themselves, their practices, and the lessons to be learned from others.

9

BEHAVIOURAL FINANCE

The Influence of Investor Behaviour

Lisa Kramer

A common refrain of late is that fear and greed drive financial markets. We hear that boom periods such as the 'tech bubble' of the late 1990s are fuelled by investors buying stocks at ridiculously overinflated prices in hopes that they can later resell to someone even greedier who is willing to pay even more. Conversely, conventional wisdom holds that during market crashes, investors panic and sell stocks en masse, causing prices to plummet even lower. These actions on the part of investors are often characterized as mistakes. Yet, according to academic research in finance, although individual investors may not always act rationally, financial markets remain 'efficient.' In recent months, we have seen market gyrations that seem grossly at odds with any notion of efficiency. Credit markets have frozen to a virtual halt, storied Wall Street investment banks have all but disappeared, massive banks have failed, world markets have plunged in an almost unprecedented manner, and policy makers have gathered in hasty attempts to stem the haemorrhaging.

In my view, there is no question that there have been extreme market events associated with panic and greed. Also, I personally believe that the current crisis has arisen in part because of the actions of financial-market professionals ranging from loan originators to Wall Street executives. The activities of such players, however, cannot fully explain the breadth and depth of this crisis, so let us consider an alternative which places some of the blame on deficiencies in our understanding of *investor behaviour*.

In his presidential address to the American Finance Association, John Campbell outlined the challenge the finance profession faces in explaining the divergence between *normative* household finance (the optimal decisions individuals should make according to the sophisticated set of asset-pricing models that have been developed in the last half-century) and *positive* household finance (the decisions individuals actually make). He argued that the discrepancy between normative ideals and positive reality can be attributed to mistakes made by investors.[1]

Of course, everyone makes mistakes from time to time. But is it reasonable to conclude that investors keep making the same mistakes and keep failing to learn from them? Might there be another reason that our financial models continually fail to capture accurately the decisions and actions of individual investors? Back in the seventeenth century, when Sir Isaac Newton thought deeply about his having observed an apple falling straight down to the ground from a tree, he found his observation to be at odds with the standard model of the world, a model that did not yet incorporate the phenomenon of gravitational forces. He might have accepted the simplistic explanation that the apple falling straight to the ground must be an aberration of nature, or a chance occurrence among the assortment of possible routes the apple might have taken to its final resting spot. Doing so might have allowed him to cling to the status quo model of the world. Instead, he questioned the model and ultimately came up with a brilliant and inspired way of improving it so he could explain the falling apple and simultaneously explain how the moon could be immune to the same fate of crashing to the earth. He incorporated gravity in his model of the motion of bodies, and in so doing he helped us all take a great leap.

We need to follow Newton's lead in finance. We have antiquated *Homo economicus* models of investor behaviour, models that characterize individuals as perfectly rational robot-like entities who make decisions only in terms of personal-wealth maximization, with no room for emotions and with no regard for considerations other than the purely financial. When individuals deviate from the 'optimal' wealth-maximizing decision, we chalk the actions up to 'mistakes' rather than question our sacred models. But there exists the beginnings of an alternate world view.

The brain, of course, is where individuals' preferences originate and where mistakes are either made or not made. And the brain is the focus of the rapidly advancing field of neuroeconomics, a discipline that combines the analytic techniques of neuroscience, psychology, and economics to explore the biological basis for economic decisions. A recent survey of neuroeconomics in *The Economist* discusses hopes that 'breakthroughs in neuroscience will help bring about the integration of all the behavioural sciences – economics, psychology, anthropology, sociology, political science, and biology relating to human and animal behaviour – around a common, brain-based model of how people take decisions.'[2]

What does neuroeconomics have to do with the financial crisis? While there is no shortage of theories about the ways in which the actions of big players – Wall Street financiers, policy makers, and regulators – may have led to the financial crisis, I contend that a careful consideration of individual investor behaviour may help us better understand how investors' reactions to market events may lead to increased market volatility, for instance, and may prolong the crisis itself. If investors act in ways that are based on preferences and inclinations rooted firmly in the brain, then we would be foolhardy to attribute all of their unexpected behaviours to 'mistakes.' Instead, we might learn something about investor behaviour, incorporate the true preferences of individuals in our financial models, and be better prepared in the future.

Investor Characteristics and Financial Decisions

Risk tolerance is at the heart of virtually every financial decision an investor makes: which types of securities to transact in; when to buy, sell, or hold; whether to rebalance a portfolio at any given point in time, etc. There is abundant evidence that an individual's level of financial risk tolerance depends on age, income and wealth, gender, and marital status. Lesser known is evidence suggesting that many additional personal characteristics are related to financial-risk tolerance, including ethnicity, birth order, education, and personality traits such as self-esteem. There is even evidence that physiological considerations such as levels of hormones and neurochemicals affect one's appetite for risk.

In spite of this, financial models do little to account for changes in risk aversion that investors may experience over time. This omission could, in many instances, lead to the false conclusion that investors make systematic mistakes. For example, suppose investors systematically tend to shun risk during the fall and winter seasons. If that were the case, then if an economic crisis were to take place during the fall, it would not be surprising to find that investors might react more strongly and sell risky stocks more aggressively than if the crisis were to happen during a period when they were more tolerant of risk. Many of the largest financial crises have occurred in the month of October: the Great Crash of 28 and 29 October 1929; Black Monday on 19 October 1987; and some of the worst market downturns in history in the financial crisis of October 2008. Is this noteworthy? Consider the following.

Psychologists have found that depressed people are less tolerant of risk, including financial risk. In a series of papers,[3] my co-authors and I hypothesize a relationship between seasonal depression, seasonal tolerance for financial risk, and economically large seasonal variation in financial markets. We cite a voluminous literature in medicine and psychology documenting the fact that in the winter and fall seasons, when daylight is scarce relative to the rest of the year, about 10 per cent of the population suffers from severe, clinical depression associated with Seasonal Affective Disorder (SAD). Additional numbers suffer from a milder, subclinical version of the same condition. With a fraction of the population becoming depressed in the fall and winter months, we conjecture that the proportion of risk-averse investors rises (since depressed individuals tend to be more risk averse). Risk-averse investors, then, shun risky stocks in the fall as the length of day shortens, and this has a negative influence on stock prices and returns. As the amount of daylight rebounds through the winter months, investors recover from their depression and become more willing to hold risky assets, which, we posit, has a positive influence on stock prices and returns. Interestingly, the seasonal variation in market returns is more prominent in countries at extreme latitudes, such as Sweden, where the fluctuations in daylight are more extreme. Further, the seasonal patterns are six months out of sync in southern hemisphere markets such as Australia where the seasons are six months out of phase. We demonstrate as well that there is an opposite seasonal pattern in safe Treasury bond returns relative to stock returns, consistent with the seasonal variation in risk aversion that we believe also underlies the seasonal patterns in stock returns. If SAD-affected investors are shunning risky stocks in the fall, as they become more risk averse, then they should be favouring safe assets at that time, which should lead to an opposite pattern in Treasury bond returns relative to stock returns. Additionally, we find seasonal patterns in bid-ask spreads on U.S. stocks consistent with the SAD hypothesis, as well as consistent evidence in the flow of funds between safe and risky mutual-fund categories: there are net flows out of risky funds and into safe funds in fall, and the patterns reverse in winter. Other researchers have found additional confirmatory evidence of the influence of SAD in financial markets by studying analysts' stock-earnings forecasts, the underpricing of initial public stock offerings, returns to real estate investment trusts, and an analysis of an expanded set of equity returns in thirty-seven countries. Collectively, this body of research implies that individual risk preferences may vary seasonally.[4]

Further evidence that investors exhibit changes over time in their taste for risk comes from a recent story in the *Wall Street Journal:* 'At one point during the day, investors were willing to pay more for one-month Treasurys than they could expect to get back when the bonds matured. Some investors, in essence, had decided that a small but known loss was better than the uncertainty connected to any other type of investment.'[5] Basically, some investors were so nervous that they drove up the price of a Treasury bill higher than its face value. These people were no longer expecting a return *on* investment; all they wanted at this point was some assurance of a return *of* investment. Standard financial models do not allow for this kind of behaviour!

While I do not for a moment mean to propose that investor behaviour *caused* the catastrophic market events of October 1929, 1987, and 2008, I do think it is worth considering that seasonally varying risk aversion played a role. Yet standard financial models leave no room for human characteristics such as risk aversion that may change over time. But there is hope. Economists expect that 'neuroeconomics will deliver its first big breakthroughs within five years' and that by then 'neuroeconomics will have uncovered enough about the interactions between what goes on in people's brains and the outside world to start to shape the public-policy agenda.'[6] Employing functional MRI techniques (in which volunteers undergo a painless brain scan while making economic decisions), neuroeconomics researchers have been able to pinpoint the regions of the brain that are involved with financial decision making. A region of the brain called the nucleus accumbens is associated with fear and reward, and it appears to be activated when individuals are making risky choices. In contrast, another region of the brain called the anterior insula appears to activate when individuals make riskless choices. Discoveries such as these imply a promising path forward, but, while the research is under way, how should investors weather the current financial storm?

Practical Advice

First, consider an investor who is planning for retirement. For the past forty-five years she has dutifully invested $1,000 in the S&P500 Index each and every year.[7] Let us consider her investment performance under two different scenarios. Under Scenario A, she has the poor timing and misfortune to invest each year at the point when the S&P500 is at its highest and most expensive point of the year. Under Scenario B, she somehow manages to time the investment of her $1,000 each year to occur at the magical point when the S&P500 Index is priced at its *lowest* point of the year, the cheapest time of the year to invest if one has the benefit of hindsight. How well positioned would this investor be under each of these scenarios, based on the relative performance of each of these two portfolios at the end of 2007? Under Scenario A, her portfolio is worth about $380,000. Under Scenario B it is worth almost $475,000, which is significantly more than under Scenario A but perhaps not as much more as you might have expected. Remember, these two values represent the extremes of her having invested at the *worst* possible time each year versus the *best* possible time each year. The *typical* (i.e., average or median) investor's performance over this period would be closer to $420,000. The point of this demonstration is that a diligent investor who plowed money into the market every year ended up with a sizable nest egg even if her timing wasn't as good as it could have been. We would all prefer to be the investor with $475,000 rather than the one with $380,000, but the vast majority of us would end up being investors with close to $420,000, and all of the long-term investors from one end of the spectrum to the other in this example ended up much better off than if they had they put their forty-five annual investments of $1,000 under a mattress.

So be as fearful or greedy as you like, *just keep saving and investing*. If you have fun trying to beat the market, enjoy doing it; just don't trade too much (those fees and realized capital gains will eat you alive), and each year make sure you keep putting money in the market.

Myself, I am a prudent investor, with a long-term investment strategy, and for the most part I stick to my plan. Some investors find it difficult to follow their plans in periods of high market volatility such as those we have experienced of late, feeling the urge to churn their portfolio holdings when prices are falling. The easy access to online trading exacerbates the problem, increasing the likelihood that an investor will succumb to the urges, urges that are totally natural by the way, and abandon the long-term strategy. For such investors, it may be wise to employ the services of a fee-only financial adviser: an individual who never accepts commissions for the products she recommends but rather charges a fixed fee for service. Such an adviser has no incentive to pander to your emotions or to churn your portfolio during periods of market volatility.

I often remind people: *know yourself.* If you are inclined to waves of fear and greed but have decided not to act on these impulses, avoid inspecting your portfolio's performance every day (or many times each day, which, again, has become commonplace in this age of the online brokerage account and easy access to real-time market data). One who has a long-term investment strategy stands to benefit very little from such frequent performance evaluations. Periodic inspection can be prudent, but a long-term investment strategy shouldn't require maintenance more than once or twice a year. The state-of-the-art research cited above strongly suggests that at least some individuals exhibit seasonal changes in their risk tolerance. It is conceivable that you may be among those who are more risk averse in the fall and winter, which would make you more prone to react in a kneejerk manner when you see drastic market movements during those seasons. So be aware. And consider doing your annual tune-up of your long-term financial plans only during periods when you are emotionally calm, perhaps the spring or summer.

Conclusion

Academic research in finance is often criticized as being out of touch with reality and at odds with the experiences of veteran practitioners. Is that surprising, given that standard financial models assume that all investors are the same automatons, leaving little room for the influence of the very characteristics that make us human? Human characteristics bear importantly on the functioning of financial markets. If investors make decisions that can be explained by reference to their personal traits, then investment advisers and the finance profession at large could use that information to better tailor efforts to educate investors on making sound financial decisions. Further, policy makers could be better prepared to respond to financial crises in ways that are constructive. Likewise, if investors make decisions in accordance with their innate appetite for risk, and if risk tolerance varies over time, then we should enhance our economic models to more fully incorporate agents' risk preferences, ensuring a closer marriage of normative and positive finance.

NOTES

1 John Y. Campbell, 'Household Finance,' *Journal of Finance,* 61, no. 4 (2006): 1553–1604.
2 *The Economist,* 'Do Economists Need Brains?' 388, no. 8590 (2008).
3 See Mark J. Kamstra, Lisa A. Kramer, and Maurice D. Levi, 'Winter Blues: A SAD Stock Market Cycle,' *American Economic Review,* 93, no. 1 (2003): 324–43; Ian Garrett, Mark J. Kamstra, and Lisa A. Kramer, 'Winter Blues and Time Variation in the Price of Risk,' *Journal of Empirical Finance,* 12, no. 2 (2005): 291–316; Ramon P. De-Gennaro, Mark J. Kamstra, and Lisa A. Kramer, 'Seasonal Variation in Bid-Ask Spreads,' University of Toronto manuscript, 2008; Mark J. Kamstra, Lisa A. Kramer, and Maurice D. Levi, 'Opposing Seasonalities in Treasury versus Equity Returns,' University of Toronto manuscript, 2008; Mark J. Kamstra, Lisa A. Kramer, Maurice D. Levi, and Russ Wermers, 'Seasonal Asset Allocation: Evidence from Mutual Fund Flows,' University of Toronto manuscript, 2008.
4 See Steven D. Dolvin, Mark K. Pyles, and Qun Wu, 'Analysts Get SAD Too: The Effect of Seasonal Affective Disorder on Stock Analysts' Earnings Estimates,' *Journal of Behavioral Finance,* forthcoming; Kin Lo and Serena S. Wu, 'The Impact of Seasonal Affective Disorder on Financial Analysts and Equity Market Returns,' University of

British Columbia manuscript, 2008; Steven D. Dolvin and Mark K. Pyles, 'Seasonal Affective Disorder and the Pricing of IPOs,' University of Kentucky manuscript, 2007; Mark K. Pyles, 'The Influence of Seasonal Affective Disorder on Real Estate Investment Trust Returns,' College of Charleston manuscript, 2007; and Michael Dowling and Brian M. Lucey, 'Robust Global Mood Influences in Equity Pricing,' *Journal of Multinational Financial Management,* 18 (2008): 145–64.

5 'Mounting Fears Shake World Markets as Banking Giants Rush to Find Buyers,' *Wall Street Journal,* 18 September 2008.

6 *The Economist,* 'Do Economists Need Brains?'

7 The choice of forty-five years is arbitrary. The lessons of this example apply equally to other investment horizons. Note that for simplicity we ignore dividends, transaction costs, and taxes.

10

Pension Management

Looking across the Abyss: Pension Design and Management in the Twenty-First Century

Keith Ambachtsheer

Our economic leadership does not seem to be aware that the normal functioning of our economy leads to financial trauma and crises ... in short, that financially complex capitalism is inherently flawed.

– Hyman P. Minsky, 1986

First, a confession. When I wrote to the pension-fund community this past summer that 'returns on most risky assets will likely be below their long-run averages for some time yet,' I was not imagining the compressed financial trauma we have been experiencing since September. As the global financial system continues to teeter on the edge of an abyss, stock prices have been rising and (mainly) falling daily by amounts that used to take years. What was originally perceived as just a Wall Street issue has now become very much the Number 1 issue on Main Street. In light of all this, the goal of this chapter is to offer perspective. Recent events need to be framed in a way that helps us and the organizations we work for make the transition from initial states of shock and trauma to constructive deliberation and, eventually, constructive action.

This chapter is divided into four parts. First, I set out a theory that explains what has caused, and is still causing, the trauma on Wall Street and increasingly on Main Street as well. The theory has been with us for many decades, articulated most clearly by an (until now) obscure American economist named Hyman Minsky. Second, Minsky's theory (the Financial Instability Hypothesis) logically leads to a plan of what needs to be done immediately to stabilize the faltering financial and real economies. Versions of this plan are now taking shape around the world. The theory also helps to identify actions that will help prevent a future recurrence of the kind of financial crisis currently under way. Next, the chapter addresses the implications of all this for pension design (part 3) and management (part 4) in the twenty-first century, and particularly for the pension-industry leaders charged with leading the way.

The Financial Instability Hypothesis

Nobel laureate Paul Samuelson once observed that many of his fellow economists seemed to have trouble coming up with operationally useful theories. It has become clear that Chicago-born Hyman Minsky (1919–96) did not suffer from this affliction. Minsky's ideas and their relevance today are set out in Randall Wray's excellent paper 'Financial Markets Meltdown: What Can We Learn from Minsky?'[1] To summarize Wray's explanation of Minsky's theory:

- The structures of capitalist economies become more fragile over extended periods of prosperity, making stability eventually destabilizing.
- Why? Because perceptions of increased economic stability allow greed eventually to trump fear, leading to a mindset Minsky called 'a radical suspension of disbelief.'
- Underlying this dynamic is a fundamentally flawed economic model variously called 'transactions-oriented capitalism' or 'money manager capitalism.'
- At its essence lies the replacement of a system of financial transactions based on personal assessments of creditworthiness with one based on a series of 'originate and distribute' transactions involving virtually no personal interaction.

- Those caught up in this form of capitalism appear to behave rationally by hedging risks or shifting them to others.
- Only in retrospect does reality set in: mass delusion propagated by the dysfunctional interplay between policy makers bent on deregulation and a financial system with strong vested interests in keeping the boom going.
- 'Irrational exuberance' follows logically from policy-induced financial innovations that promote leverage and stretch liquidity. The result is a series of price bubbles in the financial, real estate, and commodities markets.
- These bubbles eventually burst, causing havoc first in the financial markets and then in the real economy. Widespread optimism is displaced by widespread pessimism.

The history of capital markets falls nicely in line with Minsky's Financial Instability Hypothesis. In my own research into capital market behaviour, I have shown that the twentieth century divides into series of eras ten to twenty years in length, alternating between pessimistic and optimistic market mindsets. In this context, I have also been assessing the dynamics of the first era of the twenty-first century (i.e., the increasingly pessimistic 'Post-Bubble Blues Era') for almost eight years now.

Where Do We Go from Here?

With the accelerating transition of the market mindset from optimism to pessimism since September, the question needs to be asked: Where do we go from here? The logic of the Financial Instability Hypothesis suggests that we must achieve two goals: 1) minimize the fallout from the current crisis, and 2) apply the lessons learned to stand the Minsky Hypothesis on its head by devising a series of measures geared to preventing the recurrence of the kind of destructive behaviour it postulates at some future date. Some thoughts about each goal:

- **Minimize Fallout of Current Crisis**: Minsky leaves no doubt about what needs to be done immediately. He wrote that 'a financial crisis is not the time to teach markets a lesson by allowing a generalized debt deflation to simplify the system by wiping out financial wealth.' Governments must draw a fine line between allowing the guilty to suffer the consequences of their actions, on the one hand, and softening the blows inflicted on the innocent through concerted programs aimed at market stabilization, liquification, recapitalization, home-ownership preservation, and the maintenance of high employment, on the other. I note with relief that actual government responses to the current crisis around the world are becoming increasingly measured and coherent as the severity of the crisis is increasingly understood.

- **Prevent Its Recurrence**: Surely the first step in building a more robust financial model is to appreciate fully the lessons of the Minsky Hypothesis. How do we guard against the recurrence of 'a radical suspension of disbelief' about risk by financial-market participants at some future date? How do we ensure the return to, and the continuation of, credit-allocation processes based on personal contact and accountability rather than on model-based, faceless 'originate and distribute' transactions? How do we redesign regulatory processes to be consistent with the lessons embedded in the Minsky Hypothesis? And how do we redesign organizational-governance processes to be consistent with the lessons embedded in the Minsky Hypothesis?

This chapter is not the place to answer each of these questions in great detail. Suffice it here to say that I believe they are the right questions, and that there are good answers to each one of them. The far bigger challenge is to go from good 'on paper' answers to their actual implementation in the global financial system and in the vast array of organizations that comprise it. Some specific thoughts related to the pensions sector of the financial system follow.

Pension Design in the Twenty-First Century

A silver lining around the current financial crisis cloud is that it is clearly exposing the serious design flaws of many traditional Defined Contribution (DC) and Defined Benefit (DB) pension arrangements. Probably the most obvious DC design flaw is the lump-sum 'end game' still embedded in most of these arrangements, often combined with still-significant equity exposures in the pension accounts of older workers and retirees. These people have just seen a significant part of their retirement wealth disappear, with only limited prospects of recovering it. Now add falling home-equity values, and a materially lower-than-anticipated standard of living during their post-work years suddenly looms large for them. This very real, and very painful, outcome points to the urgency of attaching life-annuity transition 'end games' to pension plans that start out investing retirement savings in diversified but 'at risk' personal accounts. Age-based, automatic rebalancing formulas in pension accounts (e.g., target-date funds) can alleviate this problem to some degree, but, without life annuities, the ugly prospect of outliving one's money remains.

The design problems embedded in traditional DB plans are more subtle. Older workers and retirees are largely shielded from the direct impact of the kind of sharply falling asset prices that we experienced in recent months. Their 'losses' will likely be limited to having to forego inflation-related pension increases for some time to come. The more serious problem now lies in finding ways to fill the sizable holes that have appeared in DB plan balance sheets. Barring a miraculous recovery of asset prices, prudence requires that DB balance-sheet risk be reduced in some plans, and additional contributions to fill the holes will have to be made in virtually all plans. And this will have to be done in economic conditions likely to be ugly for years to come. Who will bear the cost of recapitalizing these DB plan balance sheets? In corporate plans, shareholders will undoubtedly bear some of this pain. But workers will not escape unscathed either. Some may lose their jobs as costs are cut in other places. The luckier workers will keep their jobs but will not get pay increases for quite some time. The economics of recapitalization work differently in the public sector, where it is easier to shift a significant part of today's cost burden unto future taxpayers and workers.

My book *Pension Revolution*[2] showed the way out of these traditional DC and DB design traps. The solution lies in dropping the opposable 'either DC or DB' mindsets that continue to dominate the pensions field, and moving on to more creative, integrative 'and-and' alternatives. Young workers need portable, cost-effective personal pension accounts that can eventually morph into life annuities. While they have many working years ahead of them, they should now have the opportunity to buy risky assets at what will eventually be recognized at attractive prices. Older workers and retirees, on the other hand, need access to regular, reliable future payment streams for life now or in the near future. An effective pension design accommodates the different needs of the young and the old in a seamless, transparent, non-conflicted manner. The current financial crisis adds urgency to the need to move to pension formulas designed with this integrative 'and-and' requirement in mind. My recent public-policy commentary *The Canada Supplementary Pension Plan: Towards an Adequate, Affordable Pension for All Canadians*[3] places these ideas in a Canada-specific context.

Pension Management in the Twenty-First Century

With retirement savings around the world now amounting to some $30 trillion, the pensions sector is a major player in the global financial system. To better understand the sector, it is useful to carve the $30 trillion into two $15 trillion halves, one 'retail' (e.g., mutual funds, insurance products, self-managed) and the other 'wholesale' (e.g., various types of pension funds). The $15 trillion 'wholesale' further divides into two $7.5-trillion halves, with one half made up of some 100+ 'LAS' funds (i.e., large, arm's-length, sophisticated), and the other half comprising the rest of the pension-fund universe. As an extension, the 200 funds ranking 101–300 in size amount to some $2.5 trillion. We might call them the 'LAS-Lite' funds.

The LAS funds, and their LAS-Lite cousins, are where the leadership of the global pensions sector resides. If pension funds are going to be managed differently in the future, it is this small leadership group and their boards (i.e., just a few hundred people) who will take the first decisions to do so. So we might appropriately ask what actions these people *should* take now in light of the current financial crisis and the Minsky insights into its origins and how future recurrences might be prevented. Here are some closing observations and thoughts:

- The LAS leadership group did not play a major direct role in the transition of financial capitalism from its traditional relationship-based form to the more recent model-driven transaction-based form that eventually resulted in the current financial crisis.
- However, LAS leaders did little to prevent that transition either. Indeed, by seeking 'higher returns at lower risk' in the wrong places, some got caught up in the Minsky dynamic.
- The question facing LAS leaders now is how active to become in transforming the current financial system into a structure less prone to the destructive dynamic so well described by Minsky. Stating the obvious, we cannot have sustainable retirement-income systems without sustainable financial markets.
- Given this direct link between the sustainability of retirement-income systems and financial markets, LAS leaders have a fiduciary obligation to play a constructive role in moving the financial system to a sounder footing.
- This role could take a number of forms. The most basic is a public commitment by individual LAS funds to their own stakeholders to manage the fund according to a short list of 'best practice' principles related to defensible investment beliefs, responsible risk management, and effective organization design. Table 1 lists seven such principles.
- A joint commitment to such a set of 'best practice' principles by a number of the globe's leading funds would be a logical extension.

- A higher level of intervention would see the LAS fund leadership actively involved in the design and creation of processes to prevent recurrences of the kind of crisis we are experiencing now. This could be done through already existing umbrella pension-sector organizations or through new, emerging networks with explicit missions to that end.

Table 10.1
The seven habits of highly effective pension funds

- The goal of a pension-investment program is to deliver target pension payments at a competitive cost over the long term in a fair manner.
- Achieving this goal requires the integration of realistic investment beliefs, the use of a broad range of investment opportunities, and a contribution rate that is both adequate and affordable.
- Risk measurement and management must fit the context of the pension program. The ultimate risk is that the pension plan fails to achieve its stated goal over the long term. Managing this risk requires controlling the extent of 'bad' outcomes over the short and medium terms, as well as actually achieving an acceptable net-risk premium over the longer term.
- Earning an acceptable net-risk premium over the longer term requires the successful dynamic allocation of fund assets between three basic 'asset classes': 1) Liability-Hedging (LH), 2) Short Horizon-Risky (SHR), and 3) Long Horizon-Risky (LHR).
- As SHR strategies are zero-sum games with an even balance between winners and losers, long-term wealth creation depends on the successful execution of LHR strategies.
- Information systems must measure actual outcomes against desired outcomes. Investment results must be adjusted for both costs and risks.
- Integrative management at this level of complexity requires good governance, high professional skill levels, and competitive HR strategies that link compensation to desired outcomes.

As this book goes to press, I am happy to report that some of these suggested interventions are already beginning to take shape. The

Network for Sustainable Financial Markets (NSFM) was born earlier this year as a virtual global think tank of concerned professionals and academics. The NSFM is already interacting with more formal national and international organizations charged with institutional and financial-markets reform. The Rotman International Centre for Pension Management (ICPM), a research centre supported by twenty LAS funds from nine countries, is actively working on devising collaborative strategies in the pensions sector that will maximize positive impact. The Council of Institutional Investors (CII) in the United States has already joined forces with the CFA Institute to intervene actively in U.S. reform efforts. They have already been in touch with the Canadian Coalition for Good Governance (CCGG) and the Pension Investment Association of Canada (PIAC) to begin to make this a multinational effort.

These are good beginnings. However, much remains to be done. What are *you* prepared to do?

NOTES

1   Randall L. Wray, *Financial Markets Meltdown: What Can We Learn from Minsky?* (New York: Levy Economics Institute of Bard College, Public Policy Brief no.94, 2008).
2   K. Ambachtsheer, *Pension Revolution: A Solution to the Pensions Crisis* (New York: Wiley and Sons 2007).
3   K. Ambachtsheer, *The Canada Supplementary Pension Plan (CSPP): Towards An Affordable Pension for All Canadians* (Toronto: C.D. Howe Institute, Issue 265, 2008).

PUBLIC POLICY

Carts and Horses and Horses and Carts: How Public Policy Led to the Subprime Disaster

Michael Hlinka

Have you ever seen a really spectacular display of tumbling dominoes? You know – where knocking over one begins an intricate, cascading pattern that ends up who knows where? That seems to describe what we're witnessing right now. The collapse of the U.S. subprime mortgage market led to a couple of highly publicized bankruptcies, which contributed to a global credit crunch and a historic sell-off in the world's equity markets. If you know what shoe will drop next, you're a better man than I am, Gunga Din.

However, even as events unfold, there is a rush to judgment to determine what caused the ongoing economic carnage. The popular interpretation seems to be that we're witnessing a colossal failure of free markets. It's Capitalism's fault and the White Knight of Public Policy, mounted on his trusty steed, Regulation, must deliver the distressed Economic Damsel from the Evil and Terror of voluntary contractual arrangements. Only one problem with that view: it puts the cart before the horse. It wasn't a free and unregulated market that's to blame for the fiasco that was subprime. To the contrary, it was a surfeit of laws, oversight, and flat-out government meddling that led to the asset bubble and the fall-out around it that has affected so many people whose only sin was that they played by the rules imposed on them.

It might not be a bad idea to define the problem precisely before we try to understand what caused it in the first place. It's really quite simple: in a short period of time, many American citizens defaulted on their mortgage loans. That's it. End of story. Which leads to a very simple follow-up question: Why? What were the unique circumstances that led to an unusually high number and percentage of defaults? Because the indisputable fact is that a decline in property values, per se, does not necessarily lead to mortgage defaults. You can't blame the default phenomenon on an asset bubble alone.

Before I get going, I feel compelled to write an explanatory para-graph about what is meant by a free market. Any economic system, market or command, operates within the framework of society's laws, regulations, and customs. That's self-evident. A free market implies that parties are able to enter into negotiated agreements, without the threat of force or any other form of coercion. If I'm stopped on the street and someone asks me for money – and I choose to give it – this is a free-market transaction. If I'm stopped and asked for money and I give it because I'm told that, if I refuse, a knife will come out – this is not a free-market transaction. Nor is it if someone stops me on the street and asks for money and I give it because I know that, if I don't, I will be knifed by the state.

The Curious Trend of Mortgage Default Rates

The Great Depression was a traumatic economic event. Along with all other financial assets, real estate crashed. It's estimated that at one time half of U.S. properties were in the foreclosure process. But after that – from the 1940s until the end of the twentieth century – the American residential real estate market enjoyed an extended period of stability. This was reflected, among other things, in low foreclo-sure rates. Yet, if we examine records from 1970 to 1999, admittedly with the benefit of 20/20 hindsight, it's impossible not to observe a trend that was a portent of things to come. Over those thirty years, 1970–99, there was a gradual yet unmistakeably steady increase in foreclosure rates ... *irrespective of economic conditions.*

The careful reader will have noticed that I italicized that last phrase. This is a technique that writers use to emphasize particularly important points. Other techniques include bolding and underlining or using an exclamation point rather than a period to punctuate … so allow me to rewrite the last sentence in the previous paragraph: 'Over those thirty years, 1970–99, there was a gradual yet unmistakeably steady increase in foreclosure rates … _**irrespective of economic conditions!**_ I stress this because even I was shocked by the data, obtained from the Mortgage Bankers Association of America. A decade-by-decade breakdown is provided in Table 11.1.

Now you understand why I got carried away with the italicizing, bolding, underlining, and exclamation pointing in the previous paragraph. From the fourth quarter of 1973 to the second quarter of 1975, unemployment rose from 4.9 per cent to 8.7 per cent. Inflation exceeded 11 per cent in 1974 and didn't fall much below it the next year. Yet foreclosure rates were actually lower than in 1971, when the economy grew at a rate of 3 per cent and inflation was under control. Even more incredibly, foreclosure rates in 1997 and 1998 – when economic growth was almost 4 per cent – were almost three times as high as those that occurred in the deep and dark recession of the mid-1970s.

How is this possible?

Time to Put on Your Steel-Toed Boots

The Community Reinvestment Act (CRA) was signed into law by President Jimmy Carter in 1977. On its surface, its purpose seemed benign: to 'encourage' lending institutions to meet the needs of borrowers in all segments of their communities. The CRA provided that all companies that received insurance from the Federal Deposit Insurance Corporation (FDIC) would be evaluated by the relevant regulatory agencies to determine if the act's criteria were being met.

Table 11.1
Foreclosure rates, 1970–99*

Year	1970	1971	1972	1973	1974	1975	1976	1977	1978	1979
Foreclosure Rate	.3%	.5%	.5%	N/A	.5%	.4%	.4%	.4%	.4%	.4%

Year	1980	1981	1982	1983	1984	1985	1986	1987	1988	1989
Foreclosure Rate	.5%	.5%	.8%	.8%	.9%	1.0%	1.2%	1.3%	1.2%	1.0%

Year	1990	1991	1992	1993	1994	1995	1996	1997	1998	1999
Foreclosure Rate	.9%	1.0%	1.0%	.9%	.9%	1.0%	1.0%	1.1%	1.1%	1.1%

* How to read this table: In 1990, for example, nine mortgages out of one thousand, or nine-tenths of 1 per cent, were in the foreclosure process at the end of the year.

Penalties for non-conforming institutions were severe. Expansion plans could be curtailed. The threat of class-action lawsuits was ever-present. The Heavy Hand of State Power came down hard and the next time the economy slipped into recession (1981–2) foreclosure rates were about twice as high as they had been during the previous slowdown. As Casey Stengel used to say: 'You could look it up!'

Let's speak honestly and plainly, even if it means stepping on a few politically sensitive toes. (I warned you to wear protective footwear.) A public-policy decision was made to pressure financial institutions to lower their lending standards. The decision was motivated by the desire to assist historically disadvantaged minorities achieve home ownership. This was consistent with the spirit of any number of affirmative-action initiatives that made their way into American life during that era.

I can almost hear the collective inhaling of breath and see the reflexive flaring of bleeding-heart nostrils ... 'How dare he!' 'Doesn't he realize ...?' Trust me, I can be as disingenuously sensitive as the next guy when it suits my purposes. But it doesn't help us understand a data series about mortgage-default rates that makes no intuitive sense. Clearly, *something* (there I go again, italicizing) had to have changed in the years leading up to the subprime bubble.

The problems were compounded with the arrival of President Bill Clinton in the Oval Office. He and his team wanted to increase home ownership – irrespective of whether or not the individual's credit history warranted it. Commencing in 1994, the Department of Housing and Urban Development launched a series of highly publicized cases against financial institutions. The onus fell on the defendants alleged with wrongdoing to prove that they were not guilty of racial discrimination if their lending practices excluded more black than white mortgage applicants. Faced with this reality – a knife poking into their backs – banks and Savings and Loans (S&Ls) responded by doing the rational thing, dropping their lending requirements ... for everyone.

And that's the important point – one that is being obfuscated in the Fog of the Rhetorical War that surrounds this issue. Some sophists turn the argument on its head and claim that this explanation 'blames' minorities for the subprime mess that metastasized into the credit crunch. That's about as valid as saying that $1 + 1 = 11$. Mr Carter is not a visible minority. Mr Clinton is not a visible minority. The majority of the apparatchiks who worked in and/or administered the various agencies from 1977 onward and exerted the pressure that ultimately led financial institutions to lower the lending bar were as white (if not pure) as driven snow. And my guess is that at the end of the day, if and when the dollar value of defaulted mortgages in the current crisis is totalled, Americans of Caucasian descent will be responsible for more than blacks and Latinos combined. This isn't about race or national origin; it's about failing to pay back borrowed money.

One final point. President Carter was a Democrat. President Clinton was a Democrat. I hope that no one is reading this, chortling delightedly, because it looks like the Party of the Donkey was primarily responsible. Because, as it happens, the jackasses and real architects of this economic fiasco just happen to be Republicans.

The Fun Really Begins

The spark that led to the conflagration occurred on 11 September 2001.

I don't know what you remember about 9/11. The memory that stays with me is that it had to be one of the most beautiful days of that calendar year. There wasn't a cloud in the Toronto sky. The late summer sun was brilliant. It was the type of day that made you glad to be alive. And the contrast between my reality and the suffering felt by so many decent families, people who had awoken that morning much as I had to a world we all believed was safe, made it just that much more poignant.

I also recall wondering what would happen next. The horror of 9/11 required a response. The United States had been attacked and there were thousands of victims. Osama bin Laden took credit for the devastation. He was reportedly somewhere in Afghanistan. It seemed entirely appropriate to bring him to justice. The world was largely united behind the military effort that culminated in the battle of Tora Bora three months later. It is believed that bin Laden slipped through the grasp of elite U.S. troops at that time and the trail grew cold. But it seems that President George Bush had his own agenda, one that was bigger than Osama bin Laden ... and it involved fighting a Global War on Terror.

Bush, however, had to bring the American people along with him. Soon after 9/11, he was asked what sacrifice ordinary Americans would have to make to fight his war and he responded: 'Our hope, of course, is that they make no sacrifice whatsoever.' Give him credit. At least he meant what he said. The implicit quid pro quo was: 'You let me do what I want, and I'll let you do what you want.' The American people, generally a kind and gentle lot, just wanted to enjoy life and an important part of enjoying life in a consumer society involves going to the mall and shopping until you are a-dropping.

To go shopping, you need money. Not to worry. In 2001 the U.S. federal government ran a surplus of $128 billion. This swung to a deficit of $158 billion a year later, swelled to $378 billion in 2003, and actually grew even larger in 2004 – $413 billion or 3.4 per cent of GDP. (By way of contrast, in 1975, at the peak of the previously cited recession, the budget deficit was $53 billion, which represented 3.3 per cent of GDP.) Yet even this fiscal stimulus wasn't enough. During the same period, the Federal Reserve Board pushed down interest rates, flooding the system with liquidity and so providing an artificial steroid-like boost to the economy.

In the aftermath of 9/11, an emergency Federal Open Market Committee meeting slashed the discount rate by 50 basis points to 3.0 per cent. That went down another 50 basis points just over two weeks later. And, from November 2001 to November 2004, the discount rate remained at or below 2.0 per cent – levels that were unprecedented. The system and its lending institutions had more than enough money to say yes to any loan request, for the artificially high supply created its own demand – and this is ultimately what led to the asset bubble in real estate, defaults in the subprime market, and the credit crunch.

If the Fed hadn't continually been pumping money into the banking system during those years, we know what would have happened. The immutable law of supply and demand would have fixed everything all on its own. When supply is limited, greater demand results in higher prices. It always does. We measure the price of money with interest rates. They would have gradually increased. This would have tempered housing prices. Banks would have been more selective about who was getting money. The bubble would never have had the chance to form in the first place.

President Bush will leave the Oval Office with the lowest approval ratings in modern history. If anything, I suspect that history will judge him even more harshly. I certainly hope so. However, there's one particularly annoying carpetbagger who's been as slick as Teflon in avoiding his fair share of the blame. Alan Greenspan was chairman of the Federal Reserve Board. If any single individual had the power and influence to prevent the bubble from expanding, it was Greenspan. Yet, even as anecdotal evidence about trouble ahead mounted, and the economist Robert Schiller sounded his warnings, Greenspan was not only as active as a deer in the proverbial headlights – he actually spoke these words in April 2005: 'Innovation has brought about a multitude of new products, such as subprime loans and niche credit programs for immigrants ... lenders have taken advantage of credit-scoring models and other techniques for efficiently extending credit ... Where once more-marginal applicants would simply have been denied credit, lenders are now able to quite efficiently judge the risk posed by individual applicants and to price that risk appropriately. These improvements have led to rapid growth in subprime mortgage lending.'

Need I say more?

Conclusion (or Putting the Horse before the Cart)

I began this chapter with a very simple proposition: the root of the subprime problem was that people who took out mortgage loans failed to repay them. Then things snowballed. It's human nature to try to figure out how to tinker with the system to prevent something like this from happening again. And, because my thesis is that faulty public policy caused this crisis, I'm going to suggest two common-sense systemic changes to prevent anything like subprime from re-peating itself. Crazy me, I want to make sure that people who get mortgages actually repay them.

First, let's rethink loan standards. The evidence suggests that cred-it has already tightened drastically. My guess is that what in some cas-es is being identified as a credit crunch may just be a more rational pricing of risk. But that's really neither here nor there. Not that long ago in Canada, the standard insurable mortgage required a down payment of 25 per cent of the purchase price and allowed for a twen-ty-five year amortization period. I'd encourage my American friends to think about those colour-blind terms as a reasonable model. (And while we're at it, the deductability of mortgage-interest payments against taxable income should be gradually eliminated.) Further, only very secure mortgages should be government guaranteed. Risk-ier loans could be granted and we should allow for private insurance – but it would be buyer beware.

More important, a mechanism is required to prevent politicians from using artificially cheap money to pay for their personal agendas. The solution is as plain as the nose on your face. Milton Friedman ar-gued years ago that there was no need for the Federal Reserve system. He wanted to 'abolish the Federal Reserve and replace it with a com-puter.' Bravo. Just grow the money supply at a constant rate – the in-crease of nominal GDP, which is about 5 per cent annually. Then let the invisible hand of the marketplace determine the cost of money. Imagine if that radical system – a truly unregulated market safe from state tinkering – had been in place in 2003 and 2004. Higher de-mand for loans would have seamlessly increased interest rates, forc-ing the bad credit risks out of the marketplace as inevitably as dumb ideas inevitably force the good ones out of the public-policy debate.

When I hear members of the political classes chatter about the current financial mess, I get a little bit anxious. I watched the last Obama-McCain debate. Both blamed the real-estate bubble on the greed of Wall Street and the greed of Washington. (What each of them really meant, of course, was the greed of Wall Street and the greed of the guys on the other side of the aisle.) Both welcomed – almost gleefully – the prospect of increased government regulation, supervision, oversight, and meddling. We shouldn't be surprised. If at their core they weren't busybodies, they wouldn't be career politicians.

What government does, and doesn't do, matters. And less is generally more. The soundest economically oriented public policy provides everyone with the widest possible latitude to negotiate freely their own arrangements. Sound public policy means that there is strong protection of property rights. Sound public policy means that there is swift enforcement of legally negotiated contracts. Sound public policy means that government doesn't try to pick winners and losers, the market takes care of that. And, most important, sound public policy requires the understanding that printing money or running deficits doesn't generate wealth. What generates wealth is people setting their alarms early, working late, and everyone realizing that production should precede consumption, that is, the horse should always be put before the cart.

Contributors

Keith Ambachtsheer is director of the Rotman International Centre for Pension Management, an adjunct professor of finance at the Rotman School of Management, and publisher and editor of the recently launched *Rotman International Journal of Pension Management*. His firm, KPA Advisory Services Ltd, has provided strategic advice on governance, finance, and investment matters to governments, industry associations, pension-plan sponsors, foundations, and other institutional investors around the world since 1985.

David Beatty is the Conway Director of the Clarkson Centre for Business Ethics and Board Effectiveness and a professor of strategic management at the Rotman School of Management. A fellow of the Institute of Corporate Directors, he serves as a corporate director of BMO Financial Group as well as five other companies. Over his career, he has served on thirty boards in Canada, the United States, Mexico, and Australia. An Officer of the British Empire, he was the inaugural managing director of the Canadian Coalition for Good Governance.

Laurence Booth is a professor of finance at the Rotman School of Management. He holds the school's CIT Chair in Structured Finance. Director-at-large and editorial board member of the *Multinational Finance Journal*, he also serves on the editorial boards of the *Journal of Multinational Financial Management* and the *Canadian Journal of Administrative Sciences*, and has acted in a similar capacity at several other journals. He is a recipient of the *Financial Post*'s 'Leader in Management Education Award.'

Wendy Dobson is director of the Institute for International Business and a professor of business economics at the Rotman School of Management. She is a research fellow at the C.D. Howe Institute, vice-chair of the Canadian Public Accountability Board, and a corporate director of TD Bank Financial Group and TransCanada Corporation. Professor Dobson is a member of the Trilateral Commission and serves on the International Steering Committee of the Pacific Trade and Development Network and on the Advisory Committees of the Peterson Institute for International Economics and the Asia Society.

Peter Dungan is adjunct associate professor of business economics and director of the Policy and Economic Analysis Program at the Rotman School of Management. He is also a member of the Ontario Economic Forecast Council.

Ramy Elitzur holds the Edward J. Kernaghan Professorship in Financial Analysis and is associate professor of accounting at the Rotman School of Management. He has been a visiting professor at the Recanati Graduate School of Business and the Stern School of Business. He has won the Rotman School's Teaching Excellence Award several times.

Jim Fisher is vice-dean, Programs, and professor of strategic management at the Rotman School of Management. He holds the school's CCMF Chair in Entrepreneurship. He co-founded the Canada Consulting Group, which later merged with the Boston Consulting Group, and served as executive vice-president of Weston Foods, chairman and president of William Neilson Ltd, and president of George Weston North American Bakeries. Four times 'Professor of the Year' in the MBA program, he has taught leadership in the degree and executive programs of the Rotman School for the past decade.

Michael Hlinka, who holds an MBA from the Rotman School of Management (1986), is an instructor, University of Toronto School of Continuing Studies, and a business commentator with CBC Radio and Television.

John Hull is the Maple Financial Group Chair in Derivatives and Risk Management, professor of finance, and co-director of the Master of Finance Program at the Rotman School of Management. He is the author of *Risk Management and Financial Institutions* (Prentice Hall, 2006), *Fundamentals of Futures and Options Markets* (Prentice Hall, 6th ed., 2008), and *Options, Futures and Other Derivatives* (Prentice Hall, 6th ed., 2006), all of which are widely used by finance practitioners worldwide.

Eric Kirzner holds the John H. Watson Chair in Value Investing and is professor of finance at the Rotman School of Management. He is the chair of the Independent Review Committee of Scotia Securities and is a director on the boards of the Equitable Trust Group and University of Toronto Asset Management Services. An external adviser to the Hospitals of Ontario Pension Plan, he is co-author of the best-sellers *Protect Your Nest Egg* (CanWest, 2006) and *The Buyer's Guide to Mutual Funds* (Penguin, 2004).

Lisa Kramer is an associate professor of finance and the Canadian Securities Institute Research Foundation Term Professor at the Rotman School of Management. An expert on the emerging field of behavioural finance, she has authored papers for many outlets including the *American Economic Review*, the *Journal of Empirical Finance*, the *Journal of Banking and Finance*, and the *Encyclopedia of Complexity and System Science*. She has given seminars on her research at universities around the world and is a regular presenter at conferences including the annual meetings of the American Finance Association, the Western Finance Association, and the European Finance Association.

Roger Martin is dean of the Rotman School of Management and holds the school's Premier's Chair in Competitiveness and Productivity. He is a professor of integrative thinking in the Desautels Centre for Integrative Thinking and is director of the AIC Institute for Corporate Citizenship. He has written seven *Harvard Business Review* articles and published two books: *The Opposable Mind: How Successful Leaders Win through Integrative Thinking* (Harvard Business School Press, 2007) and *The Responsibility Virus: How Control Freaks, Shrinking Violets – and the Rest of Us – Can Harness the Power of True Partnership* (Basic Books, 2002). In 2007 he was named a *BusinessWeek* 'B-School All-Star' for being one of the ten most influential business professors in the world. He serves on the boards of Thomson Reuters, Research in Motion, the Skoll Foundation, the Canadian Credit Management Foundation, Social Capital Partners, and Tennis Canada. He is a trustee of the Hospital for Sick Children and chair of the Ontario Task Force on Competitiveness, Productivity and Economic Progress.